I.S.B.N. No. 0 904435 06 7

1974

ESTHER THE QUEEN

by

MILDRED DUFF

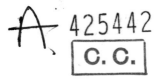
Published by
Zoar Publications, 36 Marlborough Road, Sheffield,
S10 1DB, Yorks.

Printed by
O. & M. Ltd., 1 Rugby Street, Leicester, LE3 5FF, England.

CONTENTS

Chronological note listing ancient kings of Persia:

Cyrus (550-529 B.C.) authorized the return of the Jews.
Cambyses (529-522) conquered Egypt.
Darius I (521-486) authorized the building of the Temple in Jerusalem (Ezra 6)
Xerxes (485-465) unsuccessful against the Greeks, is the king of Esther
Artaxerxes (465-424) sent Ezra and Nehemiah
Artaxerxes II & III, followed by Darius II (? Neh 12.22.) & III were feeble kings not mentioned in the Bible.

1

THE GREAT KING

I am Ahasuerus the great king, the king of the lands where many languages are spoken, the king of the wide earth, far and near!"[*]

So thought King Ahasuerus, as *"he sat on the throne of his kingdom, which was in Shushan, the palace"* (Esther 1. 2), and he liftcd his proud head higher, and looked haughtily down at the princes and nobles who sat beneath him, and knew himself to be the richest and mightiest ruler of the widest empire the world had ever known.

For in those days he reigned *"from India even unto Ethiopia."* For nearly three years his word had been law to millions of men and women; and all the richest countries, far and near, had laid their treasures at his feet.

Assyria, Egypt, Babylonia, and many a land beside, for all the grcat nations of Old Testament times, which during thousands of years had possessed powerful kings of their own, had been compelled to own him for their master, and obey the governors he sent to rule them.

It is terrible to think of one man possessing such unlimited power; his subjects bowed before him with the trembling reverence that should only be given to God. They crawled into his presence on their knees; they pretended that the sight of his

[*] These are the exact words carved in stone by the order of this powerful monarch of ancient Persia; a copy is to be seen in the British Museum. This king is generally called "Xerxes" in history; but the Bible spelling of his name follows the real sound of the old Persian more closely.

awful majesty dazzled their eyes. Little wonder that he grew proud, and overbearing, till he believed no king had ever lived who might compare with himself for splendour and wisdom.

—   —   —

A great feast is being held in Shushan, the palace. It is spread in a wonderful hall, the roof of which is supported with *"pillars of marble"*, so highly polished, that they reflect the gleaming gold of the ceiling, and the silver sheen of the curtain-fastenings, like steel mirrors. The heads of the pillars, where the gilded cornice rests, are formed of kneeling marble bulls, with horns and hoofs of pure gold; and between the pillars—which open on to a lovely garden—are gorgeous hangings of richly embroidered stuffs, tasselled and fringed with gold, and fastened *"with cords of white linen and purple"* (the royal colours of Persia) slipped through silver rings.

A pavement of many-coloured marbles, arranged in beautiful patterns, lies beneath the feet of the guests, who do not sit upright as they feast, but lean back luxuriously, on couches of gold, with silver feet, and embroidered cushions, stuffed with down.

Without, the sun blazes in a cloudless blue sky, but the hangings are drawn,and only as the gentle summer wind, laden with sweet scents from the garden, stirs them softly, does a stray sunbeam find its way into the strange, rich place; now gleaming for an instant on the golden ceiling, now glancing across a fierce-faced lion painted on the walls; now lighting up the precious pearls and emeralds with which the king's white and purple robes are richly sewn; now touching the bronzed cheeks of the king's guests.

All the great men of the empire are gathered here, "the power of Persia and Media." Their blue-black hair is carefully oiled, scented, and curled; their long beards neatly trimmed. Bracelets encircle their sinewy arms, and their stately figures are wrapped in splendid robes. On each man's head is a crown of gold; for these are the governors of all the great nations over

whom Ahasuerus reigns. They have come from the uttermost
parts of his vast empire at his commandment.

But, with all his possessions, Ahasuerus is not a contented
man. Wealth and power bring no real satisfaction. He is a
heathen, and very different from that other great king, who
understood so well where the only true content is to be found.

"I shall be satisfied," said King David, "when I awake with
thy likeness" (Psalm 17. 15). Many thousands of David's own
people are living in Persia, many hundreds in Shushan, but
Ahasuerus takes no heed of them—as yet.

Now, there is one small country which will not acknowledge
him as its master. Darius, his father, the great conqueror, had
captured country after country, until he came to Greece; and in
trying to subdue that, he was beaten back.

Lord of almost all the known world beside, Ahasuerus cannot rest because this one small country is not his also; and he
has invited all his princes and governors to this splendid feast,
that he may tell them so, and command them to help him.*

"Am I not the mightiest king in all the world!" he cries;
"and shall a small nation like this defy me? No! I will march
through all Europe, and no nation or city of the world shall
dare to resist me!"

These are his very words as handed down to us by an old
historian.

Then he bids his guests remember all the treasures he has
been shewing them for many days past; his heaps of gold; his
chests of jewels; his piles of pearls; his vast storehouses, filled
with grain; his stables of magnificent horses; his regiments of
highly-trained soldiers.

"Behold the riches of my glorious kingdom!" he cries, "is
there anything too great for me?"

And with one voice his guests answer, "Nothing, O king,
your word should be a law to the whole earth."

Their answer pleases the king, so the feasting and drinking
go on merrily.

* The Bible tells us about this feast-council, but does not give the reason why it was called, as that
has little to do with the story of Esther.

In the outer courts of the palace a great banquet has been prepared for men of lower rank; the palace consists of many buildings and courts. Beyond the garden are seen the huge walls of the "royal house." It is there that Vashti, the queen, is entertaining the ladies of her court. Persion ladies seldom appear in public, and never take part in the feasts of the men.

Rich meats, highly spiced and seasoned, luscious fruits, and red wine "in abundance" load the plates and golden goblets of the guests. No man is forced to drink, but the king drinks deeply, and most of the guests follow his example.

Drink always brings out the worst side of a man's character, and as the wine heats his blood, and clouds his brain, Ahasuerus grows yet more boastful.

"Saw any of you treasures like to mine?" he cries, leaning back in his golden throne, while young slaves serve him on their knees.

"None, O king."

"Had any monarch before me stores so vast, palaces so beautiful, slaves so numerous?"

"Not so, O king."

Then Ahasuerus suddenly remembers one treasure that he has not shown them—Vashti, his beautiful queen.

He does not love her, but he is proud of her, for *"she is fair to look on"* (Esther 1. 11), and dressed as she must be now in her festive robes and flashing jewels, with the crown royal on her head, he feels sure that all his princely guests would be dazzled with her splendour, and would cry again and again, "No king so great in all the world!"

So he cries to his seven chief chamberlains, "Go to the house of the queen, and bring her before me, that my princes and people may see her."

When Ahasuerus is sober, he is self-willed and imperious, as we shall see; but now that he has been drinking heavily all reason and justice forsake him, and he can think only of the gratification of the moment.

Yes, this is one of the terrible effects of strong drink in every age, and on every mind.

Yet even as he speaks, in spite of the wine he has drunk, his conscience tells him he is doing wrong. It is against Persian law for a woman to appear at such a scene as this. If she should refuse——?

"She dare not!" he thinks, "for am I not the king?"

2

THE QUEEN

In her own beautiful rooms with their richly decorated walls, gilded cornices, and heavily embroidered curtains, Queen Vashti feasts the great ladies of the land, the wives and daughters of the king's guests.

Young slaves, black and brown, with silver rings about their arms and necks, bear large bronze bowls of scented water to the ladies, that they may wash their hands before eating; women-slaves bring silver dishes of beautiful fruits from the king's garden; oranges, figs, pomegranates, and delicious peaches, for which the land of Shushan is famous; while rows of young girls seated on the marble floor play sweet music and sing songs in praise of the queen.

And Vashti, seated in the highest place, her haughty head crowned with the golden diadem, looks almost as proud as King Ahasuerus himself, in the "court of the garden" without.

(Strange it is to trace today in the desert dust the few poor crumbling stones of this old-time palace of Shushan.)

Suddenly the embroidered curtains that screen the door are drawn aside. Vashti looks up in surprise. Just within the doorway stand the king's seven great chamberlains, the highest officials of his court.

Solemnly they enter, walking in grave procession. Vashti knows their faces well.

They bow low before her.

"The king commands your attendance, O queen, that you

may appear before the princes of the Empire. You must follow us into his presence."

Vashti starts, and a red flush of anger mounts to her cheek.

"What! appear before the princes as they sit at their wine? Never!" she cries, and clenches her white hands together passionately.

"The king commands it," repeat the chamberlains, as though that settled the matter. It seems almost impossible to them that anyone, least of all a woman, should refuse to obey the great king.

"I will not!"

Vashti had risen at their entrance, but now she seats herself again, and her fair face grows hard and colourless as white marble, while all her ladies look at her in wonder and alarm, and the songs and music die away in breathless silence.

She has defied the king!

Slowly and sadly the king's chamberlains return to the court of the garden. They fear for the queen; they fear still more for themselves. They have failed to carry out the king's orders. One word from him would hurry them all to a cruel death.

With downcast looks they pass under the splendid hangings of the pillared hall. Arriving in the presence of the king, they fall face-downward on the marble pavement at his feet.

King Ahasuerus sees at a glance that they have failed, and his dark eyes sparkle with anger.

"Well?" he cries, in tones which make them thrill with terror.

"The Queen Vashti refuses to obey the king's command," they murmur, scarcely finding voice enough to answer.

"Refuses!" He has but just boasted to his princes that no one in the whole earth would dare to disobey him. Can he believe his ears? His authority defied in his own palace? He, the king, put to shame before all his court—and by a woman?

The thick veins in his forehead swell with the fierceness of his anger; his blood burns within him like liquid fire. It is his own self-will and the strong drink he has taken that have brought this shame on him. But he will not see.

"To disobey *me!*" he thinks, "she shall be bitterly punished," and he turns to *"the seven princes of Persia and Media, which sit the first in the kingdom"* (Esther 1. 14).

History tells us that the heads of the seven principal families of Persia—of whom the king's family was one—were the king's companions and advisers by right of birth. They alone were allowed to speak with him on a kind of equality, they alone were allowed to enter his presence whenever they chose—to *"see the king's face"* (Esther 1. 14), as the Bible says.

"What shall we do unto the Queen Vashti according to law, because she hath not performed the commandment of the King Ahasuerus by the chamberlains?" he asks in a voice hoarse with anger.

Now according to strict Persian law it is the king who has done wrong; but this stands for nothing with the all-powerful monarch and his slavish counsellors.

A king of Persia, a short while before, had wished to do a very wicked deed, so wicked that even he hesitated, and asked the wise men of his kingdom whether they would find a law for it.

"No, there is no law for it," they replied, "but a king of Persia may do as he pleases, for he is above all law."

Then the princes remembered that their own wives and daughters have heard Vashti refuse to obey her husband.

These princes are heathen, and in their hearts they despise women, as all heathen do. For it is Christ alone who teaches to the world woman's true position, making her the equal and the helpmeet of man.

It is Christ alone who shows to woman the right way in which to use her power, not like Vashti by haughty defiance, but by the pure, gentle spirit of the Saviour.

And then these princes are afraid for themselves. If Vashti goes unpunished their own wives will no longer submit to be treated as little better than slaves. They will take courage by Vashti's rebellion and stand up for themselves.

And Memucan, one of the seven chief princes, rises, and answers the king.

"Vashti the queen hath not done wrong to the king only, but also to all the princes, and to all the people that are in all the provinces of the King Ahasuerus. For this deed of the queen shall come abroad unto all women, so that they shall despise their husbands in their eyes, when it shall be reported. The King Ahasuerus commanded Vashti the queen to be brought in before him, but she came not."

And, with an air of deep wisdom, he goes on to speak of the difficulties that will arise, and says:—

"If it please the king, let there go a royal commandment from him, and let it be written among the laws of the Persians and the Medes, that it be not altered, that Vashti come no more before King Ahasuerus; and let the king give her royal estate unto another that is better than she" (Esther 1. 16-19).

The king's eyes flash angrily. There is no law for Vashti; he has but to speak, and this will be done. And Memucan tells him that when this decree is published all the women in the wide empire will honour their husbands—by which he means, fear them,—as slaves fear their masters.

Fiercely angry, and flushed with strong drink as the king is, Memucan's crafty answer pleases him.

"You speak well," he says, and all the assembled princes echo his words.

So he calls loudly for his secretaries and dictates letters to be sent to all the provinces of his vast empire, *"according to the writing thereof"*; for not only do his subjects speak many languages, but they are so far apart that even the very letters of the alphabets they use are quite different.•

So Vashti the queen must give up her power and place at a word; all the long rows of slaves who haved served her on their knees, the beautiful halls, the rich garments and royal crown are hers no longer. She is disgraced, degraded; henceforth she must pass her days in one of the cell-like rooms at the farther side of the palace.

Lives there in all the world a human being strong enough to

• We can see this in the broken ruins of the old cities to this day.

withstand this terrible king's decrees of death and punishment—to turn him from his will?

We shall see.

3

HADASSAH

Shushan the palace is some little distance from Shushan the city. The broad plains of Shushan stretch away like a rolling sea to the faint blue hills on the horizon, and in their midst an enormous mound of earth has been piled, and beaten into a great level platform, or terrace.

Here, noble buildings, glowing with gilding and rich colours, are grouped together, rising from amidst groves of graceful palms and lemon and citron trees. To the left stands the king's royal fortress, with its massive walls and dark towers; to the right, in the plain below, lies the City of Shushan.

Walls of sun-dried brick, with great gates and a hundred towers, surround the citizens' houses within; without the city are more houses, and beautiful gardens, and orchards full of fruit; and beyond these again fields of corn and millet seed, as far as eye can see.

And now, from palace, and fortress, and city, rises a busy hum of many voices, the continual passing to and fro of many feet; whilst down all the roads that lead into the city, across the great plains from the farthest corners of the empire, stream hosts of armed men.

Warriors from every land; squadrons of Persian horse-soldiers, the finest in the world; for none can ride like the Persians, who have spent at least half their days in the saddle since they were young children. Long strings of two-humped camels heavily laden, soldiers in chariots, soldiers on foot, vast stores of corn and food of every kind, all pouring into the city at the great king's command.

For the feast-council is broken up, Vashti, the proud, beautiful queen sent away in disgrace, and now the tyrant's word has gone forth that Greece, the only country that has dared to hold out against his almost overwhelming power, is to be crushed at one blow.

Far and wide across the vast empire Ahasuerus' messengers have gone, calling up the soldiers of every land, that he may march to Greece at the head of the greatest army the world has ever seen. Forty-nine nations are sending all their best soldiers in obedience to his orders. It is said in the streets of Shushan that two million men at least will follow the king.

Round the palace at Shushan runs a splendid picture of these men in richly coloured tiles let into the wall. They seem to march in stately procession; they carry long spears in their hands; bows and great quivers of arrows hang at their backs; their robes are embroidered in turquoise, blue, amber, rich chocolate, and snowy white, and each man looks as proud and dignified as an eastern prince.

"I will sweep across Greece like a whirlwind, I will overwhelm it like a raging flood," cries Ahasuerus in his pride and vainglory.

The Bible does not describe this unjust war, for it had nothing to do with the history of God's people; but yet from the Bible we can discover just how long it lasted.

Ahasuerus called his council-feast in the third year of his reign (Esther 1. 3). Vashti was sent away, yet the king did not choose his new queen until the seventh year (Esther 2. 16). He could not do so before. He was from home, unjustly trying to force the Greeks into becoming his servants; but trying in vain. The story of the wonderful courage of the Greeks, and of the fierce anger and amazement of the Persian monarch at his failure, you should all read for yourselves in the history of Greece.

So Ahasuerus comes back to Shushan the palace, dissapointed, hungry for the pleasures and splendours of his beautiful palaces, and more overbearing and tyrannical than ever.

Now all this while, in a humble dwelling, quite apart from the splendid halls of kings and queens, but yet on the great platform of Shushan the palace, lives a young Jewish maiden named Hadassah.

She is an orphan, and were it not for her kind cousin, Mordecai, she would be very desolate.

Mordecai is a humble attendant in the palace of the great king, and Hadassah keeps house for him, for she is his adopted daughter, and they love each other like father and child.

Many long years before Hadassah was born her people lived in Jerusalem, the holy city of God, but the cruel king of Babylon came and carried them away captive and they lived as strangers in a strange land.

The kingdom of Babylon is part of the mighty Persian empire now, and the Persians are not altogether unkind to the Jewish people. Yet they are suspicious of them, and look upon them as foreigners who are hardly to be trusted.

But Mordecai and Hadassah are faithful and patient, and never forget the God of their fathers, nor that beautiful holy city so far away.

Hadassah lives at home very quietly. She prepares the food for her adopted father, and keeps his rooms neat and clean, and his brass and copper dishes bright.

She dresses very simply, and winds her silky black tresses round her head without any ornament; and her long dark eyes are the softest and sweetest and truest in the world. "Yes," thinks Mordecai, "She is well-named Hadassah—that is 'Myrtle'—for she is fair and pure as a fragrant myrtle-spray fresh from the fields."

As Hadassah stands on the southern platform she can look down into the city and see the people passing to and fro, the citizens with their leathern coats and felt caps, the nobles and courtiers robed in flowing garments and cloaks of crimson, black,or grey. Sometimes she even catches a glimpse of the great king as he sets forth from his palace in gorgeous procession; his chariot drawn by milk-white horses and gleaming with gold, whilst all the people bow low before him; and perhaps she thinks:—

"How strange to be one of those great nobles and speak to the king face to face; how strange to be the queen and see him every day!"

Then she remembers what Mordecai has told her of Vashti's disgrace, and she whispers, "Yes, and terrible also. Oh, far better to be a humble maid as I am than to be a queen and come to such bitter sorrow!"

Then she thinks of her own people, her countrymen who are scattered through this strange land just as the prophets had foretold. They are far from their own land, at the mercy of strangers who neither love nor understand them, very often they are in danger and distress. Hadassah's dark eyes fill with tears as she remembers it all.

But one day Mordecai returns to his peaceful home with startling news. All the fair young maidens in the land are to gather at the palace that from among them the king may choose his new queen.

"The king's officers are even now setting forth to search the country far and wide, Hadassah," he says, fixing his eyes on her fresh young face.

She looks up wonderingly. "The king can make whom he will queen?" she asks.

"Yea; the maid who pleases him best shall wear the royal crown." And still he looks at her so earnestly that she wonders more and more.

"Why do you gaze at me so? Am I —Oh, no—no, that cannot be—surely they will not come for *me* also to stand before the king?" and she rises to her feet, pale and trembling.

"Yea, for you also, Hadassah," Mordecai says gravely. But Hadassah blushes and trembles sadly—the bare thought of such a thing fills her with alarm.

Mordecai is right; before many hours are past the officers from the great king's court appear before the open doorway of his humble dwelling. Whatever their demands may be, he must obey cheerfully. No man in all the broad empire would dream of resisting the officers of the king.

"In the name of the king we demand that the maiden . Hadassah be given up to us," they proclaim.

Mordecai hastens to meet them, but Hadassah shrinks back trembling, and draws the corner of her head covering across her face like a veil.

"The king shall be obeyed," answers Mordecai, bowing low; and turns to Hadassah and strives to comfort her and give her courage.

But his heart is full of trouble. She has been to him as a daughter, and never again shall her sweet presence gladden his home. If the king so decree, she shall reign a queen; yet if she is rejected she must not return to him, but must pass the rest of her life shut up in the palace away from all the world.

Be sure he tells her not to forget the God of her fathers, nor the people of her own land, in this great change that has come into her quiet life.

And Mordecai kisses and blesses Hadassah, and she is taken away.

Among broken carvings, and heaps of rubbish,and shattered fragments of marble and stone, we may faintly trace today, on the ruin mounds of Shushan, the path Hadassah trod so long ago, when she was taken to the "house of the women" in Shushan the palace.

A few fragments of marble mark the site of "the court of the garden" where Ahasuerus held his royal feast. The noble towers, wide terrace, and broad stone steps leading to the "king's house" (that part of the palace specially sacred to the king) are but heaps of earth and brick and broken tile. Beyond this again are those dim outlines in the dust that faintly indicate the noble space of ground on which the huge "house of the queen", the "palace of the women" stood.

Dust and earth and broken stone, all silent witnesses to the wonderful truth of the Bible story.

—   —   —

Hegai, the king's chamberlain, is governor over the house of the women at this time; to him are entrusted the maidens from among whom the king will choose his new queen, and to Hegai Hadassah is brought.

Many maidens have gathered here from all parts of the empire, and the rows of small chambers in which they are to lodge until the king sees them, are almost full.

Hegai is weary of apportioning to each girl her clothes and her food, the quantities of perfumes and ointments she requires, and the slaves to wait on her. Now there is yet another to provide for.

To Hadassah, who had seen so little of court life, Hegai appears almost as great as a king, with his flowing robes and great gold bracelets, and attendant slaves; but directly Hegai's eyes rest on this maiden he sees she is different from all the rest.

For the others are all gaudily dressed, and wear many jewels, and laugh and chatter, and boast of all the fine things they will do; for each believes she will be chosen queen; but this maid stands meek and quiet in her simple dress; her eyes downcast, her hands crossed on her breast.

This is no vain young girl, longing for the idle splendour of a Persian queen's life, but a modest, true-hearted maiden, fair and sweet, because she is good.

And he turns to her gently and speaks kindly to her; and to her he gives the best place of all (Esther 2. 8, 9).

At the back of the royal halls in which the queen will live are the rows of narrow chambers where the maids must pass their year of waiting. To the largest of these Hegai leads Hadassah.

In all her simple life she has seen nothing so fine before, for the tiled walls flash with colours, and the polished pavement is smooth as glass beneath her feet, and by the couch of precious wood, stuffed with down, are ranged stands, stored with alabaster vases filled with precious ointments and sweet odours, such as the Persian ladies use.

Seven serving-maids are to wait on Hadaasah; to prepare her

1. Women on a tea-plantation in the N. Iranian province of Gilan near the Caspian Sea.

2. Bas relief at Persepolis, where the remains of Darius' palace rivalled the greatest buildings of Egypt.

food and take care of her garments; and before Hegai leaves her he says:—

"How call they you, fair maiden?"

"Hadassah," she answers, in her sweet, low voice; but she does not tell him her fathers name, or that she is a Jewess, the daughter of a despised race; for, *"Mordecai has charged her that she should not show it"* (Esther 2. 10).

"You are too fair and bright for such a name," answers her new friend. "You shall be called 'Esther,' that is, 'Star,' for indeed you are a star in the court."

Now "Esther" means the same as "Ashtaroth," the old idol goddess of beauty, whom the heathens named after a star; and so a maiden of God's people becomes known by a heathen name.*

How changed her life is! Shut up in close, heavily-scented rooms, fed on the choicest fruits and white palace bread, with slaves to fan and wait on her, she is really a prisoner, and must not even speak to her adopted father, although she knows that he walks every day before the court of the women's house to inquire after her welfare (Esther 2. 11).

So for twelve months Esther lives in the palace. Many things she has to learn. Many words full of vanity and deceit she is obliged to hear; the palace slaves flatter her, and most of the people round her are living in luxury and idleness, yet her mind is all unspoilt; she is still a pure bright star.

And now the maidens are beginning to be called before the king, one by one. Each, in turn, is allowed to ask for whatever she may choose of rich clothes and jewels, and emerald clasps, and strings of splendid pearls.

One by one the maidens go, each quite sure that the king will make her queen, and loudly planning all the splendours she will indulge in, the feasts she will give, the jewels she will wear.

One by one they are rejected and sent to another part of the palace, there to be little better than slaves for the rest of their lives.

* In Persia at this time court favourites always received new names when entering the palace.

But Esther sits quietly in her chamber; she makes no outward preparation, she utters no loud boastings; but possesses her soul in patience; if it is God's will she will be queen; if not, that is God's will also.

And at last the call comes for her.

It is Hegai, the king's chamberlain himself, who tells her, and he says:—

"Ask of me what you will, Esther, and it shall be brought to you."

But she answers, "I desire nothing save what you have already given me."

And they all wonder at her, so queen-like does she look in her simple robe.

"I am ready," she says, and her face turns slowly pale, while her eyes glitter like two stars.

And thus she goes before the king.

4

ESTHER THE QUEEN

And so at last Esther passes into the presence of the all-powerful king; the man whose lightest word can condemn her to a life of hopeless slavery, or place on her humble head the royal crown of Persia.

There is expectation and keen anxiety among the palace servants.

All who have known Esther, from Hegai, the grand chamberlain, to the humblest slave, are eagerly hoping that the king's choice will fall on her—on her the fair and gentle maiden who is so thoughtful for others, so forgetful of self.

"It is the month Tebeth (December) that is the 'good' month," they whisper. "May it prove good to her!"

Perhaps in their poor blinded fashion some of them even pray for her. The more thoughtful Persians were not idolaters at this time, that is, they did not bow down to idols. Yet they were ignorant of the true God, though they believed in a mysterious spirit, whom they called "Ormazd."

But Mordecai goes about his work as usual, and no man guesses the deep anxiety of his soul, nor the silent prayers to the God of his fathers with which his heart is filled.

And God is good to Esther. Ahasuerus has become utterly weary of the painted and perfumed ladies of Persia, all alike gaudily dressed and laden with jewels; and when his eyes rest on this simply-robed maiden, with her modest step, and gentle look, he feels at once that she is fairer and purer and wiser than all the rest; therefore, when she would fall at his feet, he raises her up, and speaks kindly to her, and loves her above all the women (Esther 2. 17).

And thus, she who but yesterday was a humble girl with nothing she could call her own, today becomes the greatest lady in the largest empire of the world.

The royal crown is placed on Esther's head; she is mistress now of the whole "house of the women," with its splendid halls, its caskets of pearls and sparkling jewels, its heaps of gold, and store-rooms of costly garments. Crowds of slaves await her orders, and before her all the other women in the palace must bow until their foreheads touch the pavement.

And the king commands that a great feast shall be held in honour of his new queen, *"even Esther's feast"* (Esther 2. 18).

Thus, throughout all the palace, Esther, "star of the court," is honoured and loved, throughout all the country too—for King Ahasuerus loves her so much that he wishes her name to be a household word in the homes of all his subjects, so he orders a *"release to the provinces"* (Esther 2. 18), that is a release from paying taxes for a time.

Taxes are very grievous things in this Persian empire. There are great roads to maintain in good order, and many castles and forts to keep in repair. Ahasuerus is extravagant and selfish; spending vast sums in building magnificent palaces for himself, and in giving gorgeous feasts; and besides all this, his army is the largest and most expensive in the world.

So the farmers, and the workers of all kinds, are continually being called upon to pay heavier taxes, to send more men to the army, and thus their burdens grow greater year by year.

Now, for a while, they are to pay no taxes at all, to send no more men to the army, and all for Queen Esther's sake. How they rejoice!

Besides all this, the king gives splendid gifts to his friends, armour and jewels, and costly robes of purple and scarlet, the finest in the land.•

• Old histories tell us that Persian monarchs of this time generally gave presents to their friends at times of special rejoicing. All through the Book of Esther we find this wonderful exactitude in describing the ancient Persian customs.

But all this grandeur, honour and flattery, does not make Esther conceited, or selfish, nor forgetful of the good man who brought her up as his child. Though a great queen, with a whole nation at her feet, she still *"does the commandment of Mordecai"* (Esther 2. 20). She still obeys him as an affectionate daughter should, and Mordecai's gratitude to God is deep indeed.

It is Mordecai's daily duty to serve Ahasuerus by helping to keep watch and ward at the "king's gate." He is still but a humble servant, and no one suspects his relationship to the lovely young queen.

The "king's gate" is a great building, leading to the king's own rooms. It is necessary to guard it very strictly; for in these rooms the king sleeps, and he would be at the mercy of any enemy who succeeded in passing the gate.

Many servants keep watch here, among them Bigthan, and Teresh, two of the king's chamberlains.

In the days to come Ahasuerus will be killed in his own palace, by his own servants,* but though some of them are planning his death even now, God's hour has not come yet, and this time God will save him.

For Mordecai, quiet and watchful, soon suspects that all is not right with Bigthan and Teresh. They are for ever whispering together; their eyes are troubled, and it is easy to see that evil thoughts possess their minds. At last he discovers it all; they are plotting to murder the king; they will stab him whilst he sleeps; unless Ahasuerus is warned at once, it will be too late.

"But how make my story believed—how reach the king? I dare not go before him unless I am sent for."

Then quick the thought comes to him. Esther shall tell him! For the king loves Esther so much that he sees her every day.

How does Mordecai give Esther the startling news? Perhaps he sees the sweet young queen alone, and she calls him "father"

* Ahasuerus made bitter enemies among those around him. When he had reigned twenty years, the captain of his bodyguard conspired with a chamberlain and murdered him as he slept.

as she used to do in that old simple life of hers which already seems so far away.

And Esther thinks, "I will tell my lord the king that it is through his servant Mordecai's watchfulness that this wicked treachery has been discovered; then will the king honour him as he deserves to be honoured."

So, when next the king sends for her she appears before him all eagerness and excitement, and quickly tells her story.

"Thy servant, Mordecai, who sits in the gate, it is he who has discovered the wickedness of these men," she says. But the king is filled with such fury and wrath in an instant, that he pays small heed to her words; with wrath and fear also, for he perceives at once the terrible danger in which he has been.

Bigthan and Teresh are seized and tried. The story is true; they intended to murder the king while he slept; they are swiftly condemned and led out to die, the king's secretaries writing an account of the whole plot in the State records, as they do of every important event.

But Mordecai, whose faithful watch has saved the king from a terrible death—Mordecai sits in the king's gate still, a humble servant in spite of all Esther has said, his faithfulness and watchfulness are alike forgotten.

5

HAMAN

And now Ahasuerus strives, in a life of sinful idleness and pleasure, to forget his late defeat and humiliation in the Grecian war.

His time is spent in planning new amusements. When he should be attending to the affairs of the kingdom, and the needs of his people, he goes hunting; or passes the day in eating, drinking, and playing at dice with his slaves and flatterers.

The king's hunts are great affairs. There are fierce lions in the mountains, and antelopes and wild boars in plenty on the wide plains. The king rides to the hunting-ground in a carved and gilded chariot, drawn by white horses, trapped in purple and gold; a great knife hangs by his side, and a slave bears his bow and arrows.

When a beast appears, it is well understood by the princes and courtiers attending him, that the king is to have first shot. Should a man dare to draw his bow before the king, he would be condemned to death.

When not inclined for hunting, the king lounges on embroidered cushions in his palace, and plays at dice. Large sums of gold and silver rapidly melt away; more dreadful still, men and women-slaves are gambled for, and often won and lost on a single throw. He sleeps, and eats, and drinks to much, and altogether he leads a very selfish, useless life.

But why does not Esther, the good and wise queen, try to

turn his thoughts away from all this self-indulgence and sinful idleness?

Alas! just now she can do nothing; the king will not listen to her at all.

Ahasuerus, like all his people, has been taught to think that women are inferior to men. He still loves her in his selfish fashion; but she is only a woman, and all his confidence is given elsewhere.

He has a new favourite; his vain mind is wholly under the influence of an artful man, who knows just how to flatter and serve him in the way he loves best.

By cunning words, and great pretence of devotion to his service, Haman, the Agagite, has won the king's friendship. He understands his master's vain and indolent character, and works on this knowledge to gain his own ends.

Haman is not one of the seven chief princes of Persia; and by Persian law he has no right to a great position in the State; yet he persuades the king to give him the greatest place of all.

No doubt he says, "Oh, great king, the care of this world-wide empire is too great for you. Should so glorious, so god-like a king spend all his days in painful toil and weariness?

"Let my lord place part of the burden on my shoulders. I will execute all my lord's will; taxes will I gather, tribute will I speedily collect, traitors and rebels will I terribly punish. Whatsoever the king commands that will I do. Does not my lord know that I live but to obey him?"

Then Ahasuerus remembers that the kings of Assyria always had one chief ruler, or prime minister, who, next to the king, was the greatest man in the kingdom; he talked to the king almost as to an equal, and managed all the most important affairs in the State.

Assyrian carvings show us that it was the custom among kings at this time to make one man ruler over the whole nation, with authority so great that the king alone was his superior. This man is generally pictured standing beside the king, most richly dressed. He is the chief adviser, and though not a warrior, takes command even of the king's generals.

Ahasuerus listens to the cunning temptation. He will do as the king of Assyria did. How much trouble Haman will save him! And Haman is advanced above all the princes of the empire (Esther 3. 1).

See where he comes, his gorgeous robe stiff with gold, golden ear-rings weighing down his ears, great gold bracelets on his arms, his hair and beard curled and oiled and scented like the tresses of a vain woman.

Slaves attend him, and a self-satisfied smile flickers round his cruel mouth, for all the palace servants and guards fall flat on their faces before him, as though the sight of his dazzling splendour strikes them to the earth.

Kings have always been greeted in this fashion in Persia, but only quite lately has such an honour been paid to Haman. The king has commanded that it shall be so. Haman is to be "reverenced," to be worshipped. It is the king's decree. There lives not a Persian who dares to disobey.

No, not a Persian; but Mordecai is a Jew. Must he fall on his face before this bad, cunning man? Must he give to a fellow-creature the worship that should only be paid to God?

He cannot. To do so would be to deny the God of his fathers, whom his people worshipped in Jerusalem, the Holy City. He has been a faithful servant to the king; he saved his life, although that is forgotten, but in this, let what will come, he cannot obey. Ambassadors from Greece to one of the kings who succeeded Ahasuerus refused to bow themselves in this manner, much as Mordecai did. "It was not their custom," they said, "to worship men." The Persian king forgave them because they were not of his country. So Mordecai bows not (Esther 3. 2).

Haman holds his head so high that he does not see him, but the servants at the king's gate are quick to notice the omission.

They do not understand Mordecai; he is reserved and quiet, and never joins in their idle talk or careless laughter; so they set him down as a proud man.

"He holds himself above us, and yet he is only a servant like the rest of us. Let us see what will happen if he continues to disobey the king's decree. Is he so great a man that he dare defy the king?"

And they go to him where he sits in his place, silent and watchful. *"Why transgressest thou the king's commandment?"*

Mordecai knows only too well the terrible risk he is running; he knows the cruel, revengeful spirit of the man he is refusing to honour; from time to time dark whispers of terrible tortures inflicted within the palace walls, of lingering deaths, too horrible to be described, have come to his ears; a word from Haman and the worst of these deaths would be his. But he will not, he cannot, act against his conscience.

"I am a Jew," he says gently, "I may not do this thing."

But they laugh scornfully. "We will see how that excuse will help you when it comes to Haman's ears!" And after a while they go to Haman, like the treacherous self-seekers they are, and tell him all.

As Haman listens, his cruel lips close tightly over his white teeth, and a dangerous light gleams in his gloomy black eyes. "A Jew! A wretched bondman! What punishment is great enough for such insolence as this?"

One horror after another rises in his mind, but they are all too little. The suffering of a whole nation would hardly satisfy the bitter spite, the murderous revenge, with which his wicked soul is filled.

Then he remembers that in the time of Ahasuerus' father, a great massacre of the Magians—that is, men of the priest-class—had been carried out. On a set day every Magian who could be found had been murdered. Had not night fallen over the blood-stained cities, not one Magian would have escaped.

"Ah, this was revenge indeed! I, too, will appoint a day, and on that day every Jew throughout the land shall die. Yes, Mordecai, there shall not a soul of your people live to boast of what you have done. In the name of your nation you have defied me, then, with you, your whole nation shall perish! I have spoken!"

Yet cruelly eager as Haman is to be revenged on Mordecai and his people, one thing holds him back for awhile.

He is a heathen, and therefore very superstitious, thinking

more of "signs" and "omens" than he does of his religion. To him magic is much more important than prayer, to him "fortunate" and "unfortunate" days are more to be depended on than the power of God.

Again, in spite of the almost unbounded influence he has gained over the selfish heart of the king, Haman knows it will be difficult to carry out his terrible scheme of vengeance. And he thinks—

"I must go to work very warily with the king, or he will not consent; for affairs must be so managed that the whole massacre takes place in one day, otherwise these Jews will fly from town to town, and many escape. Yes, all the nations must rise on them at one time, and kill, and kill, until the sun goes down, even as the Magians were killed. A day of rejoicing that will be for me! Mordecai would not fall on his face before me—well, his whole nation shall lie low at my feet! Yet, if after all the king should not consent?" Haman's heavy eyebrows draw lower over his eyes at that thought, and many plans for deceiving Ahasuerus rise in his cunning brain.

At last his face clears. "I am very rich—thanks to my own cleverness"—he thinks, "and the king is greedy for money. Yes, he will consent. Now to find out a fortunate day for the work."

Then he calls the heathen priests, and they cast Pur, that is, the lot, before him (Esther 3. 7).

It is the month Nisan, the "month of opening," because it is the beginning of the summer, and the lots are cast to discover the day and month which are likely to prove most favourable for the design Haman has in his mind.

Casting the lot in Persia is supposed to have resembled dice-throwing. The priests as they threw asked if a certain date would be lucky, and then read the answer, "yes" or "no," according to the words or figures that came uppermost on the dice cubes.

Deep down in the ruins of Shushan the palace a small square object was discovered, each side being engraved with a different number of dots, much as dice are to-day.

With eyes full of eager cruelty Haman watches the casting of the lot. Again and again it is thrown, again and again he is disappointed. Not this month, nor the next, nor the next? His face grows darker and fiercer with every throw.

At last! The thirteenth day of the twelfth month ("Adar"—that is, "dark"). Haman clenches his teeth; he has nearly a year to wait.

God has overruled the casting of the lot. God is giving Haman a long space of time in which to repent of his great wickedness. Only a man in whose heart all mercy and human feeling has been quenched could maintain his dreadful purpose for a year.

But no ray of mercy is to be found in Haman's heart. He uses the time only that he may make his terrible purposes more sure.

And he smoothes his face, and arranges his golden ornaments and puts on a look of great wisdom and profound respect as he goes before the king,

Not a word does he say of his anger against Mordecai; no, the real reason of his conduct does not appear at all; he is much to artful for that.

The king bids him speak, and he begins at once; as full, apparently, of zeal for the king's affairs alone, as the most honest and upright servant that ever monarch had.

"Oh, great king, there is a certain people scattered abroad and dispersed among the people in all the provinces of thy kingdom; and their laws are diverse from all people; neither keep they the king's laws: therefore it is not for the king's profit to suffer them" (Esther 3. 8).

Not for the king's profit! Oh, the cunning of these words!

"The words of his mouth were smoother than butter, but war was in his heart: his words were softer than oil, yet were they drawn swords" (Psalm 55. 21).

And Ahasuerus thinks, "What an honest friend and faithful adviser I have in Haman! His whole mind is filled with zeal for my service."

So Haman, watching the effect of his words, gathers courage, and he says:—

"If it please the king, let it be written that they may be destroyed."

Haman knows this to be a critical thing to say; he knows that the king will feel alarmed; not so much at the idea of wholesale bloodshed, as because many of the Jews are well-to-do, and their destruction would prove a real loss to the State; it would be a loss in taxes to himself, and he needs so much money.

But Haman understands the king thoroughly, and in his wicked cunning knows exactly how to win his master's heart, and he goes on with the air of a man who is willing to sacrifice everything for the king's service.

"And I will pay ten thousand talents of silver to the hands of those that have the charge of the business to bring it into the king's treasuries."

Ten thousand talents! Nearly three and a half millions sterling of our money. Ahasuerus is struck with astonishment and admiration. Did ever king have a more faithful friend? It would not be possible to love and trust such a man too much! And he takes his precious signet—the signet of the royal seal of Persia—and puts it into Haman's hand, and says:—

"The silver is given to thee, the people also to do with them as it seemeth good to thee."

Haman's wicked heart beats thick and fast as his fingers close on the royal signet. Now indeed revenge is sure! With the king's signet in his hand he has the power of the king.

Haman was not the only man whom Ahasuerus treated thus generously. When on his way to Greece he stayed at the house of a rich man who received him with great hospitality, and who, after a while, offered to give him five and a half millions sterling—a greater sum even than Haman had promised. Ahasuerus, delighted, bade him keep his money, and then gave him a present which made his fortune still greater.[*]

Forth from the king's presence goes Haman, his heart on fire with wicked joy, and he calls for the king's scribes, the men whose special duty it is to write the king's letters to the rulers and governors of the cities and provinces of the empire.

[*] From the Greek historian, Herodotus.

They are learned men and ready writers, and amongst them is to be found the knowledge of most of the languages of the world.

It is Haman who plans the letter to the king's lieutenants and governors, but they are sent out in the king's name and sealed with the king's signet. For Persian kings at this time *sealed* instead of *signing* State documents.

"To the rulers of the king's provinces. Destroy, kill, and cause to perish, all Jews, both young and old, little children and women, in one day."

An awful decree indeed, a decree which cannot be altered, from which in Persia there can be no appeal. By command of the king!

6

MOURNING AND WOE

As soon as the letters are written, Haman sends out the posts, that is, swift messengers, to carry them to every corner of the empire; and his wicked heart rejoices, for he knows the Persian posts to be the best in the world.

On the broad roads which run from one end of the empire to the other, men and horses are stationed at regular intervals: a man and a horse for each day's journey.

Leaving the king's palace, the horsemen dash away at full speed; all day they ride, arriving at nightfall at the first rest-house along their several roads. They spring from their horses, hand the letters to the next "posts," who are already mounted and waiting, and who, in turn, speed away at once. Neither drenching rains, nor burning sun, nor black darkness, nor even a snow-storm—a rare event, greatly dreaded by the Persians—may be used as an excuse for pausing an instant. The king's business goes before all.*

So the messengers fly swiftly through the land; and the governors of many provinces read, and wonder a little, but never dream of disobeying.

They will be ready at the appointed time; they will publish the decree. On the thirteenth day of the "dark" month all the Jews in the land shall be destroyed. None shall be spared, neither grey-haired elder nor stalwart youth; the mother shall

---

* This account of the Persian postal-system in the time of Esther is taken from Herodotus, the Greek historian.

die with her infant in her arms, the fair, innocent maidens, the pretty, dark-eyed children—all shall perish.

In our own days we still hear of cruel massacres of the Jewish people, but no one man has power now, thank God, to order such wholesale slaughter as this!

Think of the awful terror that falls on ten thousand homes when that decree is made known! "Can we not escape? Can we not fly before the 'dark' month comes?"

Yet whither can they go? They are hemmed in on every side, surrounded with enemies. To try to escape will but hasten the end. And many cry, "There is no hope, no hope save in God."

Then they remember how selfish they have been, how forgetful of the Holy City, and the brave souls who are struggling to rebuild it. They have been willing to stay behind, to make homes for themselves in this heathen land. It has been so much easier to remain, so much more comfortable. Oh, they are justly punished! And they cry:—

"Oh, God, forgive us! Oh, Lord, save us! See how we weep, how we mourn before Thee; we have clothed our limbs in sackcloth, we lie in ashes, we fast until our cheeks are hollow, we weep until our tears run down even to the ground. Oh, Lord, remember Thy people!"

The decree of death has gone forth, Ahasuerus cannot recall it even if he would; but Haman gives him no time to think.

Wine stifles the conscience, deadens the mind, weakens the will, and Haman and the king sit down to drink (Esther 3. 15).

For many days Ahasuerus has not even spoken to his fair and wise queen; he thinks only of Haman now, and of his cunning flattery, while the maddening red wine that Haman leads him on to drink, has quite stolen away his senses.

We have seen how Mordecai risked torture and death rather than act against his conscience; quite calmly he has since then kept his place at the king's gate. If it is God's will that he should suffer for his faith, he will meet his fate with the dignity and courage of a martyr. But wicked and revengeful as he knows Haman to be, he never suspects the dreadful truth until

3. Sassanian relief from Naghsh-e-Rustam in Fars province.

4. Bas relief at Persepolis. Glazed brick bas-reliefs in vivid colours from Shushan (modern Shush) may be seen today in the Louvre.

the decree is published in Shushan, and Mordecai perceives all that is done (Esther 4. 1).

Then he understands that his whole nation is to be sacrificed, the land is to be stained with his people's blood from end to end.

And on his account too—because he resisted the tyrant! He cannot bear it, his heart will break; all his heroic calmness, his quiet dignity, is swept away in a flood of grief.

In agony he leaves his post. He rends his clothes. He puts coarse sackcloth on his limbs, and strews ashes on his head, and, wild with horror, goes out into the midst of the city with a loud and bitter cry (Esther 4. 1).

There is perplexity and doubt in the streets of Shushan the city; Haman's power is great with the king, but Haman is not loved by the people. They must obey though. Haman is not acting in his own name, but in that of the king, and in Shushan the city the king's voice is as the voice of a god.

So, throughout all the land, there is wailing, and weeping, and terror too great for words.

But, the first dreadful outburst of grief over, Mordecai turns back wearily to the king's gate, his kind face has grown old in a few hours.

"Go back!—go back! You cannot enter at the king's gate clothed in sackcloth; no sign of mourning is permitted within the palace," cry his old companions at the gate, barring his way. And Mordecai stands without the gate, dumb with anguish.

But it so happens that some of Queen Esther's servants see him standing there, and knowing how often she has sent greetings to the good old man, they run to her with the news.

"Gracious lady, gracious lady, Mordecai, whom thou knowest, stands without the gate, and he weeps, and sackcloth clothes his limbs, and his grief seems very great."

Esther has had trouble and anxiety herself of late, the king has taken an evil man for his friend, and is neglecting his sweet young wife. So little does she know of the king's plans, that she is quite ignorant of the decree against her people.

She is exceedingly grieved to hear of her old friend's sorrow, and she sends her servants to him with fresh robes, and bids them take his sackcloth away. Much as Esther longs to comfort him, it would be quite against the custom of the court for her to go herself.

"Gracious lady, he will not receive thy gift," cry the servants, returning quickly.

Then Esther knows that terrible trouble must be threatening; never before has she known her foster-father give way to despair. She sends, therefore, for the chief officer of her court, Hatach, one of the king's own chamberlains whom Ahasuerus has appointed to attend on her, and she bids him to go to Mordecai.

"What is it—why does he refuse all comfort?" she says, her sweet eyes full of trouble, "go to him, bid him tell me his grief."

Hatach is of high rank in the court, and is allowed to pass in and out of the king's gate as he pleases, and he comes to Mordecai.

"The queen would know the cause of your sorrow, O Mordecai," he says, very gravely; he is a man of dignity and position, and Mordecai's haggard face, and wretched ash-strewn garments, are in great contrast to the chamberlain's scented locks, and smooth features, and spotless robes.

But Mordecai cries eagerly—

"Yea, tell her—tell her that my people are sold, that Haman has promised to pay a great sum of silver into the king's treasuries, so that all the Jews in the land may be destroyed!"

Then he snatches a piece of writing from beneath the rough folds of his sackcloth, and thrusts it into Hatach's hand.

"Behold the copy of the decree that was given at Shushan to destroy them! Show it to Esther, declare it unto her, and charge her that she should go in unto the king to make supplication unto him, and to make request before him for her people!"

Hatach takes the writing, and goes, and Mordecai thinks, "Oh must not I, who brought all these innocent souls into danger, strive to save them? Yea, though in doing so I risk the life of her who is to me as my only child."

Hatach returns quickly to the "house of the women," and gives the writing into Esther's hands, telling her as he does so all the words of Mordecai.

Esther had expected bad news; but she had never dreamed of anything so terrible, so heart-breaking as this. The rich colour leaves her cheeks, and her soft eyes grow hard with horror, while she sits on her golden chair as pale and cold as a marble statue.

"My people—Oh, my people!" she wails. Then, with a thrill of utter fear she remembers Mordecai's message to herself.

"Death—it would be certain death for me to interfere! Oh, has he served so long in the palace, and does he not know? My death would not help the people. Ah! dear friend and foster-father, grief and bitter weeping have bewildered thy mind."

And she turns hastily to Hatach, the chamberlain.

"Go, Hatach, return to Mordecai, say thus unto him: *"All the king's servants, and the people of the king's provinces, do know, that whosoever, whether man or woman, shall come unto the king, into the inner court, who is not called, there is one law of his to put him to death, except such to whom the king shall hold out the golden sceptre that he may live"* (Esther 4. 11).

Then she remembers that Mordecai does not know how anxious and sad she has been of late, how fearful that the king loves her no longer; he does not guess how many proofs she has had that Ahasuerus would rather drink with Haman, the artful flatterer, than listen to her words, and so she adds very sadly:—

"But I have not been called to come in unto the king these thirty days."

—   —   —

In the dust of "Shushan the palace," the dim outline of all its great halls and wide courts have been traced. The "House of the Women," it is found, was a great building, with many chambers under one roof. At one end was a door leading to the "Court of the Garden," at the other a long passage passing through to the "King's House," and then to the "Inner Court," all exactly as described in the Bible.

Now, of all the palace this "inner court" of the "king's house" was the most strictly guarded. No one might enter there without special permission from the king. The Persians treated their monarchs as though they were gods, and the "inner court" of the palace was to them as sacred as the most holy part of a temple.

Mordecai has not forgotten this; but he believes with all his heart that God is calling on Esther to speak for her people. For this the Lord has raised her to the throne. Should she refuse, she would be a traitor to her nation, an unfaithful servant to the God of her fathers. Besides, she also is Jewish; if the king loves her no longer, as she fears, the palace walls will be no protection; she will be dragged out to die with the rest.

"Speak to Esther the queen, tell her my words, Oh, Hatach, *'Think not with thyself that thou shalt escape in the king's house more than all the Jews.'* "

But even as he speaks the sorrowful words a light flashes into his tear-dimmed eyes, and he straightens his weary limbs beneath their load of sackcloth. God will not let His chosen people perish at the hands of that bad man. Ah! no; yet if Esther and himself do not perform their parts bravely, God will raise up other deliverers, and will punish them for their want of faith. And it is with a firm voice and steady countenance that Mordecai goes on:—

"For if thou altogether holdest thy peace at this time, then shall there enlargement and deliverance arise to the Jews from another place; but thou and thy father's house shall be destroyed: and who knoweth whether thou art come to the kingdom for such a time as this?" (Esther 4. 14).

Esther was not the only woman living in the palace of the Persian kings, who was asked to take her life in her hands, by entering the inner court of the king's house unbidden.

In the days when Ahasuerus' father was a young man, the man sitting on the throne of Persia was suspected of being a usurper, of having murdered the true king, Smerdis, and artfully taken his place. It was difficult to prove whether he was Smerdis or not, for there were many circumstances in his favour; but at last a nobleman of Persia, named Otanes, recollected that if the king was not Smerdis, but Gomates the Magian priest, as was supposed, he had lost his ears. Yet here again Otanes and his party were baulked. They had no secret friends in the palace, the king would see scarcely anyone, and as it was the fashion in Persia to wear the hair in a bushy mass of curls, it was impossible at a distance to tell whether he had ears or no.

But Otanes had a daughter living in the "house of the women," and at last he sent a message asking her to find out for him. She replied that it was impossible. He sent again, and more urgently; this time she answered him much as Esther answered Mordecai: "I will obey you, notwithstanding the danger; being, indeed, well assured that if he have no ears and discover me in endeavouring to know this, I shall instantly be put to death."

Otanes' daughter was asked to break through the same court regulations as was Esther, and she feared the same fate as Esther the queen.

The second message comes from Mordecai, and now Queen Esther raises her drooping head, and the colour comes back to her face, and her dark eyes are as full of faith and courage as Mordecai's own. Her hesitation is over. She will dare all—she will *act!*

"Return to Mordecai yet again, Hatach," she says, "and these are my words to him: *'Go; gather together all the Jews that are present in Shushan, and fast ye for me, and neither eat nor drink three days, night or day: I also and my maidens will fast likewise; and so will I go in unto the king, which is according to the law.'* "

Her clear voice falters a little as she pledges herself to face that awful danger. She has lived in the palace for several years now; during that time many faces, familiar to her have disappeared; men led away secretly to death or imprisonment at a word from the king. There is no appeal against him, and he is

* Herodotus

tired of her; he no longer cares to be with her—a whole month has passed and he has not seen her face.

But her people—the poor women, the little children—must the streets be piled with their bodies, the earth soaked with innocent blood?

Oh, no—no—no! She will be strong, she will face the worst, she will fast and pray, and leave the rest with God!

"If I perish, I perish"!

Her clear voice is steady now and she stands full of simple dignity and saintly courage, as she speaks those brave words, and Hatach bows his head in silence, and passes out to do her will, awed by the martyr-spirit that thrills in her voice and lights up her eyes.

Fasting and prayer—the two always went together—it is thus that Queen Esther seeks strength and wisdom for the perilous part she has to play in the hour of her utmost need.

Mourning and wailing and woe throughout the land. "The days draw on, the time comes ever nearer, and yet there is no one to help us. O God of Israel, save Thy people!"

Fasting and tears and hands held up to God for Queen Esther's sake in Shushan the city: "Lord have mercy on Esther Thy handmaid. O Lord send Thy angels to comfort and strengthen her!"

Fasting and weeping in the queen's chambers in Shushan the palace. "Not according to the law, O Lord, but Thy laws are greater than the laws of men. Nevertheless, unless it be Thy will to save me, my death is very near. Yet will I go in to the king, and if I perish, I perish."

7

NOT ACCORDING TO THE LAW

Fasting and prayer! Esther and her maidens sit low upon the pavement. The queen's hair is unbound; no crown decks her head; her royal robe is laid aside; her eyes stream with tears, her hands are raised to Heaven in an agony of supplication; her pale lips move in ceaseless prayer.

A strange scene this to be taking place in the gorgeous palace of a queen of Persia! Mourning and woe are not supposed to enter there. The king's words break many hearts; but no grief must be shown in his presence.

So has she sat, so prayed and fasted, during three days; for the lives of many people are trembling in the balance.

At length she rises to her feet; the time of preparation is over, the hour of action come.

"Rise my maidens," she says, "bring to me my royal apparel, and the crown of gold which it pleased the king to give me; and so will I go unto the king."

Her maidens hasten to obey. They bring bowls of perfumed water, they draw ivory combs through her long dark hair, and gather it into place; they clothe her in fine white linen, and throw the royal robe of rich dark silk across her shoulders; last of all, they set the golden crown upon her head. They are so pale and affrighted, so fearful that they shall not see her again, that their trembling fingers can scarcely hold the combs or fasten the clasps of her dress.

When all is ready they stand for a moment gazing at her with tear-dimmed eyes.

Even now the king is sitting in that sacred "inner court"; the time has come; she must go.

Her maidens sink once more to their knees as the chamberlain lifts the heavy curtain and she passes from the "house of the women" into the forbidden part of the palace.

A long corridor is before her. How changed are her thoughts, her feelings, since first she saw this corridor with its tiled walls and inlaid floor!

Then she was a simple maiden, coming for the first time before Ahasuerus. Then, if she had failed to please him she would have been sent to another part of the palace to live as a slave; no greater evil could then have befallen her, for she was obeying the king's command. Now she is disobeying a law of the court; if she fails to win the king's grace she must die.

Ah, and then she was fresh and fair; the king likes new faces; she was new to him then; now she is pale with sorrow; now he is already tired of her. "Oh, be with me, God of my fathers!" she murmurs.

No one to stand between the doomed people and their fate, save this solitary praying girl. One woman against the whole power of a vast empire!

Steadily she passes down the corridor; enters the inner court.

She sees the king on his golden throne, the high crown on his head, the long sceptre of gold held stiff and still before him. Unless he holds it towards her she must die.

He raises his eyes; he looks full upon her face; and a great silence falls on all the chamberlains and servants who are standing about him; for his next words may end her life.

But Esther knows that the God of her fathers is with her in this awful moment; and the light of her noble soul shines through her eyes and her pale features glow with courage and self-sacrifice. Her life, her death, are in God's hands.

Never before has the selfish king, surrounded by selfish courtiers, seen such an expression on a woman's face.

"And the king held out to Esther the golden sceptre that was in his hand" (Esther 5. 2).

She draws nearer. She touches the top of the sceptre—she is saved!

Among the ancient Persian pictures, carved on the walls of palaces that are now crumbling ruins, may still be seen many which represent the king seated on his throne, his sceptre held stiffly before him in his right hand.

These sceptres are very long; like slender staffs, with carved and rounded tops. In the ruined palaces of Assyria the wall pictures show us sceptres on which the remains of red paint can still be faintly traced; "red" generally stood for gold at this time.

And Ahasuerus, still looking fixedly at Esther, feels the influence of her pure spirit strong upon him so that for a brief space Haman's false face and artful flatteries are quite forgotten. And he says:—

"What wilt thou, queen Esther? and what is thy request? It shall be even given thee to the half of the kingdom" (Esther 5. 3).

But Esther has prayed very earnestly to God, and God has given her wisdom, and patience, and self-control. She makes no sudden demand on the king. He would be startled, angry; by doing so she would lose all.

She brings no "railing accusation." Haman is the cruel enemy of her people; by his cunning lies and artful scheming he has led the selfish, indolent king to doom a whole people to death. Yet she does not complain of him behind his back. She is too honest, and brave, and straightforward for that. No, she will meet him face to face, and, with the Lord's help, will win Ahasuerus back to the paths of justice and duty in Haman's very presence.

And she says, *"If it seem good unto the king, let the king and Haman come this day unto the banquet that I have prepared for him"* (Esther 5. 4).

Her answer pleases the king. Haman is a pleasant companion, and his friend; the queen's thought is a good one. Of course, Ahasuerus knows that she has not yet asked the gift she would have of him. But that will wait awhile.

And he calls to his servants, bidding them tell Haman to haste with the business he has on hand, for the queen has summoned him to feast with her.

Esther receives Ahasuerus with deep respect, and Haman courteously, and the king looks long at her. The new beauty shining in her eyes, the beauty of courage and self-sacrifice, quite subdues him. Without knowing why he feels that no gift could be too great to bestow on such a woman, and again he says:—

"What is thy petition? and it shall be granted thee: and what is thy request? even to the half of the kingdom" (Esther 5. 6).

But Esther looks at Haman's cunning face, with its self-satisfied smile, and in her heart she knows that the time has not yet come. God will show her when to speak; she must be patient and wise for her people's sake.

So she answers the king as before:—

"If I have found favour in the sight of the king, and if it please the king to grant my petition, and to perform my request, let the king and Haman come to the banquet that I shall prepare for them, and I will do to-morrow as the king hath said" (Esther 5. 8).

Tomorrow; she will speak tomorrow.

8

HAMAN'S WIFE

Haman's heart is filled with selfish joy, and his mouth with boasting, as he comes forth from the queen's feast.

"I am indeed a man of power and wisdom; I am born to great things! The king has raised me to the foremost place in the State, and now the queen is giving a feast in my honour. *'Let the king and Haman come to the banquet that I shall prepare for them.'* Not for the king only—for *me* also.

"Queen Esther values me as she ought. Queen Esther sees that I stand next to the king. There is no man to compare with me in all the wide lands of the empire."

As he passes from the "king's house" into the fortified "king's gate" he holds his head higher than ever; his almost royal robes and long, curled hair, scenting the air all round him as he moves.

Within the shadow of the king's great gate sits Mordecai the Jew. His cheeks are hollow, his eyes dim with grief and fasting. Save that his pale lips move in constant prayer he sits as still as a figure carved in stone.

There is a quick bustle among the other watchers and chamberlains. "Haman comes!" All rise hastily, and as the all-powerful favourite strides haughtily towards them they throw themselves on their faces at his feet.

Mordecai hears the rustle of Haman's silken robes, catches the gleam of his golden ornaments, smells the sweet odours that are wafted from his hair and garments. Yes, this is Haman, the enemy of his people.

And they would have him worship this bad man as though he was divine! As well might he do reverence to one of the idols of this heathen land.

He will not. His people are condemned; he is brought very low; but the brave spirit within him is all undaunted still.

Calmly he sits there and steadfastly he meets the look of bitter hatred which Haman fixes on his face.

But Haman's vain heart swells with anger. Will nothing break this man's spirit?

"What! lord of all Persia as I am by the king's favour, have I no power over this wretched Jew?"

In the heat of his rage he sets his teeth, and clenches his hand, and makes a swift movement as though he would strike Mordecai in the face.

"Nevertheless Haman refrained himself" (Esther 5. 10). He does not strike the unshrinking Jew; nor order his slaves to bind and scourge him. No, no, his passionate anger would not be satisfied with such punishments as these.

Today Queen Esther practised self-control that she might save the lives of her people. Haman *refrains himself* that he may be more deeply revenged.

He goes home; he sends hastily to his chosen friends, and to Zeresh his wife. Rage and spite and wounded vanity nearly choke him.

The friends come; worldly self-seekers, who cling to Haman because he is rich and powerful, who flatter him and drink with him, greedily hoping that some of his wealth will fall to their share.

Zeresh, Haman's wife, comes also.

"Zeresh" means "the golden," and, indeed, she glitters with gold and jewels; broad bracelets encircle her bare arms, a gold circlet rests on her head, heavy gold ear-rings weigh down her ears. Her hair is arranged in rows of little curls, her face daubed with red and white paint; her half-shut eyes are artfully lengthened with touches of dark colour; and her garments are even more strongly scented than Haman's own.

And Haman looks round at his friends, and looks on his wife, and his pride bursts forth in a passion of vain-glorious boasting.

"How glorious are my riches!" he cries. "My treasure-chests are filled with gold, my rooms with silver, jewels and rich garments abound in my house; a hundred slaves wait upon my will!"

Haman is indeed rich. The king's foolish confidence in him has given him the mans of acquiring vast wealth. He can tax the poorer folk as he pleases, and no rich man would dare to refuse him anything.

"Who among you have so great a multitude of children? Ten sons call me father. Whom does the king delight to honour but me? I am the king's friend, his adviser; he has promoted me to the chief place; he has advanced me above all his princes and servants. Who, then, is so great, so glorious as I in all the land?"

"He speaks truth; he is very great!" cry his flatterers.

"Yea, very great," echoes Zeresh his wife.

"Haman said moreover, Yea, Esther the queen did let no man come in with the king unto the banquet that she had prepared but myself; and to-morrow am I invited unto her also with the king" (Esther 5. 12).

And he flings his arms wide open as though they were wide enough to seize and hold all the world.

Then suddenly he drops them to his side again, and his loud voice sinks to a fierce whisper.

"Yet all this availeth me nothing, so long as I see Mordecai the Jew sitting at the king's gate."

No happiness is possible to a wicked self-centred man. Power, wealth, all count for nothing. Haman has millions of money, titles and honours more splendid than any other man. But a greedy mind is never satisfied; the more it has the more it craves for. Haman has all the world can give, save the one thing which he would never have missed unless he had been told of

* Every Persian prided himself on the number of his sons. It is even said an annual prize was given by the king to the Persian who could show him most living sons. —Herodotus.

it, but, lacking that, everything else is spoiled for him.

A man's happiness does not lie in his riches and grandeur, but in his heart, in his soul. Mordecai, sitting at the king's gate, forlorn, despised, with the dread of a calamity weighing on his spirit, is a far happier man than Haman in his gorgeous home, surrounded by slaves and flatterers; for Mordecai trusts in God.

What a confession for Haman to make! He cannot help brooding over a fancied injury; his whole life is spoiled because one poor Jew resists his imperious will.

And what does Zeresh "the golden" say?

We have just seen how *one* wife is acting in Shushan the palace today. Her whole soul is fixed on winning her husband back to the path of justice and honour; how brave are her thoughts; how self-restrained her words; how self-sacrificing her whole conduct! What does this other wife say?

Her husband is asking for her advice, asking how far he shall carry his revenge. Surely her woman's heart will incline her to mercy?

And Zeresh and his friends say unto him, *"Let a gallows be made of fifty cubits high, and to-morrow speak thou unto the king that Mordecai may be hanged thereon."*

A "gallows!" that means a great stake of wood. Zeresh, Haman's wife, suggests that Mordecai shall suffer death by one of the cruellest methods ever invented.

Mordecai is to die with the rest of his people when the "dark month" comes; but Haman will not wait for this. He is to have this fearful instrument of torture erected at once. His eyes long to see the man who has resisted him led to a shameful death, and Zeresh his wife puts his wicked thoughts into words.

"Then go thou merrily with the king unto the banquet," she adds with a light laugh.

Merrily. Foolish woman! Can a man be merry with murder in his heart?

But the thing pleases Haman, and he calls to his servants, and causes them to set up a great stake, seventy-five feet high, and he thinks—

"Tomorrow I shall be free of this plague! Tomorrow mine enemy shall die a shameful death. Oh, would tomorrow were come!"

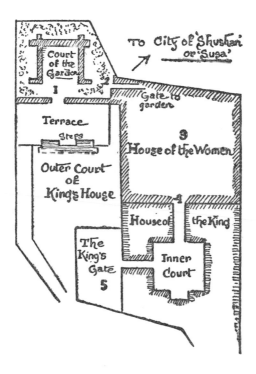

Plan of part of Shushan the palace, showing how it was arranged in the days of Ahasuerus and Esther. 1. The hall in which Ahasuerus gave his great feast. 2. The entrance through which the chamberlains passed to summon Vashti to the king's presence. 3. Where Esther lived. 4. Corridor between the "house of the women" and "house of the king." 5. Fortified gate, where it was Mordecai's duty to keep guard with other servants of the king. Put together from traces still to be seen in the dust of Shushan the palace.

9

THE HAND OF GOD

It is night in Shushan the palace. A hush has fallen over the busy city in the plain below, and the great halls of the palace lie dark and silent under the starlight.

Stay—one lamp twinkles faintly from the king's house. Who should be wakeful there at this darkest hour of the night—the hour before dawn.

"On that night could not the king sleep" (Esther 6. 1). His couch of gold, his pillows of purple and fine linen, cannot soothe him to rest. Though his subjects treat him like a god, he has no power to command sleep to visit him. He is as helpless in God's hands as the weakest child—the poorest slave; and the Lord has removed sleep from his eyes.

At last he can bear the weary tossing to and fro no longer; and raising himself on his elbow, he commands his watching slaves to bid his scribes *"bring the book of records of the chronicles."*

This book was a sort of State diary, a record of daily events written by scribes specially trained for the purpose.

Herodotus the historian writes of this custom of the Persian court in the days of Ahasuerus.

In the dead of night, by the feeble light of flickering oil-lamps, the chronicles are read before the king.

The scribe's voice soothes Ahasuerus; he leans back on his pillows, and listens with half-closed eyes.

The minutes pass; far away in the eastern sky appear the first faint streaks of pale light heralding the dawn of a new day.

And the scribe reads on:—

"In this day Bigthana and Teresh, two of the king's chamberlains, the keepers of the door, sought to lay hands on the King Ahasuerus. And the thing was known unto Mordecai, who told it unto Esther the queen, and Esther certified the king."

Ahasuerus' half-shut eyes open suddenly, and he raises his head a little, listening with closest attention.

"And when inquisition was made of the matter, it was found out; therefore they were both hanged on a tree" (Esther 2. 23).

The scribe lays down the roll, and takes up another, clearing his throat to begin a fresh record. But the king holds up his hand. The story of the conspiracy is not finished. He has listened to the punishment of the guilty chamberlains, but what of the reward to the man who saved the king? And he says:—

"What honour and dignity hath been done to Mordecai for this?"

Something, of course, has been done, only just now he cannot recollect it.

We learn from the old historians that in Persia at this time anyone who discovered a conspiracy against the kimg, or did him any special service, was given the title of "Royal Benefactor," and received large rewards besides. It was the king's business to apportion the reward according to the value of the service done. If a "Royal Benefactor" were forgotten, or poorly rewarded, it would leave a lasting slur on the king's name and government.

"Then said the king's servants that minister unto him, There is nothing done for him" (Esther 6. 3).

Ahasuerus' face flushes with anger, and his eyebrows contract into a heavy frown. His name will be a byword to all nations, if this thing is known! This very day—nay, this very hour the disgrace must be wiped away!

He looks round hastily. The lamps burn low; the pale light of earliest dawn is creeping into Shushan the palace; the shadows of night are melting away. Already there is the echo of foot-steps and the low murmur of voices in the outward court of the king's house.

And the king calls to his servants, *"Who is in the court?"*

It is Haman.

Feverish and excited, he cannot rest until his hate is satisfied. With the first streak of dawn he has left his bed. Directly the king awakes he will gain his consent to Mordecai's death.

The stake of torture is already in its place. As he stands waiting in the court, he can hear the strokes of his slaves' hammers as they drive in the last nails. A dreadful smile spreads over his face as he listens. The wretched Jew will trouble him no more.

The king's consent—nothing now between him and his vengeance save the king's consent—and when did the king refuse him anything?

The king's chamberlains look out.

"Behold, Haman standeth in the court."

"And the king said, Let him come in."

Haman's wicked heart beats high. The moment he has longed for has come!

Last night the king could deny him nothing, today will be the same. There is none to come between him and his vengeance. Ere the hour of Esther's banquet, Mordecai will be dead.

But directly Ahasuerus sees Haman he begins to speak to him on the matter that just now is nearest his heart. He has neglected the man who preserved his life. There are many people in his kingdom who would gladly see him dead; if this story of the king's ingratitude is told abroad, who will make any effort to save him?

Something specially impressive and magnificent must be done for this Mordecai. Haman is clever, Haman will advise him what it shall be.

And he says:—

"What shall be done unto the man whom the king delighteth to honour" (Esther 6. 6).

Haman's eyes flash. "This for me! Fresh titles, fresh riches, fresh honours. *For to whom would the king delight to do honour more than to myself?"*

Even revenge is forgotten for awhile in the splendid prospect he sees opening before him.

What shall he ask for? What is the greatest honour it is in the king's power to give? What would make him appear most magnificent in the eyes of the people of Shushan this day—this day on which Mordecai is to die, this day, when he is to feast for the second time with Esther the queen?

A daring thought strikes him. Yes, he will make it a day of glory and triumph indeed! And he says:—

"For the man whom the king delighteth to honour, Let the royal apparel be brought which the king useth to wear,• and the horse that the king rideth upon, and the crown royal which is set upon his head."

Haman's heart swells with pride as he says the words. How the people will shout to see him. Ahasuerus himself would not receive a nobler welcome!

"And let this apparel and horse be delivered to the hand of one of the king's most noble princes, that they may array the man withal whom the king deligteth to honour."

The princes of Persia have not been pleased at Haman's advancement over them (Esther 3. 1), and he thinks, "They shall be humbled before me, they shall be forced to wait on me as though I were indeed king!"

And he goes on, *"and they shall bring him on horseback through the street of the city, and proclaim before him, Thus shall it be done unto the man whom the king delighteth to honour"* (Esther 6. 8, 9).

Blinded by his vanity and selfish greediness Haman pours out his words, piling honour on honour. So absorbed is he in the splendid vision he has called into his mind, that he scarcely looks at the king. But Ahasuerus thinks:—

• Herodotus tells us that it was against the law for anyone to wear clothes that had been worn by the king; but the king had power to overrule this.

"To reward the man who saved me thus, would indeed redeem my character in the eyes of the people!"

"Make haste, and take the apparel and horse as thou hast said, and do even so to Mordecai the Jew, that sitteth at the king's gate."

Mordecai! Haman stands as one thunderstruck. Can he believe his ears?

"Let NOTHING *fail of all that thou hast spoken."*

There is that in the king's voice as he gives the order that chills the furious heat of Haman's passion, and checks the rebellious words upon his lips.

Haman bows his head and goes forth without a word, in silent, deep mortifcation to do the king's will. Too well he knows that all his riches and splendour depend on his master's favour. For his life he dare not disobey.

He takes the royal robe, the crown of honour, he sends for the royal horse, he seeks Mordecai. "Ah!" he mutters between his teeth, "and at this very hour I had thought to see him led to his death!"

Patiently Mordecai sits in the shadow of the king's gate; still faithfully doing his duty to the king who has caused such a load of sorrow to fall upon his heart.

He is a wise man; he has seen the great stake standing ready for use before Haman's house; he knows the bitter hatred Haman bears him, the unbounded influence Haman has obtained over the king, and he thinks, "Haman seeks my life."

Looking up he sees Haman coming slowly toward him.

"Yea, thither he comes; he has obtained the king's consent that I should die. The stake before the court of his house is for me. The Lord's will be done."

Haman comes nearer. Stands before him. What is this? He bears in his hands a beautiful robe, a crown of honour, such as only the greatest princes are permitted to wear!

Mordecai's calm look of resignation changes to one of utter astonishment. Haman, his cruel, relentless enemy, is beckoning him to rise, is holding the royal robe towards him as though about to cast it over his shoulders!

A sudden light breaks over Mordecai's bewildered senses, and he remembers the court custom—"to the men whom the king desires to honour they offer the Median robe—that is, the court robe." •

"This is from the king! The king desires to honour me, who have been cast down even to the dust. Oh, this is the Lord's doings, and it is marvellous in my eyes. Yea, the Lord is with his people still."

(In the court of Persia today some of these ancient customs are still followed. The Shah gives a cashmere robe, that has been worn by himself, as the highest reward to his most faithful servant.)

Had Haman been in Mordecai's place how his pride and vain-glory would have burst forth; how boastfully he would have triumphed over his humble enemy! But neither by word nor deed does Mordecai add to Haman's misery, as, with trembling fingers, the proud court favourite arrays the poor Jew in the splendid robe and crown.

In silence, calm and dignified, Mordecai receives the honour; in silence Haman bestows it. But his heart is hot within him; his white lips are drawn tightly over his clenched teeth; his fierce soul is unspeakably humiliated. Outwardly calm, he rages within like a hungry tiger whose prey has been snatched from his grasp just as he was about to tear it to pieces.

Yet he is but suffering as he had meant others to suffer. Just so had he planned to humiliate the princes of Persia. "The proud princes hate me because the king has set me over them. Well, they shall lead my horse through the streets of Shushan the city, in the sight of all the people." The evil he had designed for others has fallen on himself.

Now the king's beautiful white horse is led forward, its arching neck and small head richly ornamented with bosses and flowers, and trappings of gold. Mordecai is lifted to its back. He accepts the honour. His heart is filled with wonder and thankfulness. It is the Lord who has turned his shame into glory.

• Herodotus

And Haman takes the horse's golden bridle in his hand and passes slowly down from the great mound of earth and stone on which Shushan the palace is built, into Shushan the city.

How people stare to see the great Haman leading another man's horse! How they point, and laugh, and crowd about him!

Rough country fellows, in coats of coarse grey felt, driving their laden asses before them, stop to gaze and wonder. Camel-drivers, bringing in tribute from distant parts of the empire, point him out to their companions, and in languages that are strange to him seem to speak of his disgrace.

"Thus shall it be done unto the man whom the king delighteth to honour" (Esther 6. 11).

The words almost choke him.

"Thus shall it be done unto the man whom the king delighteth to honour."

Again and again must he proclaim it.

The multitude increases, crowds follow the procession. There is not a man in Shushan the city this day who does not see Mordecai's triumph. To Haman it seems that his dreadful task will never be done.

"Thus shall it be done unto the man whom the king delighteth to honour!" This man who, if Haman had his will, would be dying now in shame and agony.

At last it is over. The whole city is ready to make a hero of Mordecai, but he has no mind for feasting and rejoicing. The doom of death still hangs over his people, and he slips away from the excited crowds and quietly returns to his work, coming *"again to the king's gate"* (Esther 6. 12).

The Lord has given him honour before the people, and his steady soul is filled with deep gratitude. Yes, the God of his fathers will still protect His chosen: He will not leave them to perish in this strange land. For his countrymen's sake Mordecai rejoices that the king has thus honoured him and abased the Jew's enemy.

But what words can tell of the shame and fury in Haman's heart?

His proud spirit is crushed. His false courage gone. He is defeated, disgraced, cheated of his revenge in the very hour that it appeared most sure. He cannot bear it! He who but yesterday carried his head as high as the king is ashamed to show his face in the streets, and he *"hasted to his house mourning, and having his head covered"** (Esther 6. 12).

There, before his door, grim and ghastly in the morning sunlight, stands the dreadful stake of death. Haman turns his head away, and hurries over the threshold. How changed are his thoughts since he crossed it in the earliest dawn this morning!

He sends hastily for Zeresh his wife; he sends for his false friends, who have flattered and followed him only because he is rich; he sends for the pretended wise men who have so often encouraged him with their wicked advice and cunning words.

Then he stands up before them all, his gorgeous robes soiled with the dirt of the streets, his face distorted with anger and shame; a dull, cold fear stealing over his soul that the days of his glory are ended.

Then tells he *"Zeresh his wife and all his friends everything that had befallen him"* (Esther 6. 13).

With looks of alarm they listen to his hurried words, and Zeresh turns pale as death beneath the paint on her face; and with one voice they cry out on him:—

"If Mordecai be of the seed of the Jews, before whom thou hast begun to fall, thou shalt not prevail against him, but shall surely fall before him" (Esther 6. 13).

Bad counsellors are poor comforters; they advised Haman to do wrong; now, when they see he is in danger, they declare his cause hopeless and that nothing but utter ruin lies before him.

---

* To cover the head was a sign of mourning and disgrace.

10

ESTHER SPEAKS

"And while they were yet talking with him, came the king's chamberlains, and hasted to bring Haman unto the banquet that Esther had prepared" (Esther 6. 14).

Hurriedly Haman makes ready for the feast; but his mind is full of gloomy foreboding, and Zeresh watches him with doubt and dread in her heart. She has no thought to bid him "go in merrily" unto *this* banquet.

But Esther receives him graciously, and the king treats him as usual; and presently, as he sits in that beautiful hall, with its rich pavements and glowing walls, and breathes its soft air, sweet with the scent of hundreds of garlands of flowers, while young slaves fill his golden cup with strong red wine, he half forgets his fears.

He drinks deeply—as, indeed, does the king; for to drink great quantities of wine is one of the bad customs of the Persian court. •

As the wine mounts to his brain Haman's courage revives. The queen is to beg a boon of the king today; perhaps, when she has spoken, he also may speak; and Mordecai may yet be disgraced in some way. Yes, all may yet be· well. He is the queen's guest, the king's friend. He stands alone, and above all the princes of Persia.

• The ancient historian Herodotus, writes: "The Persians are very fond of wine and drink it in large quantities."

His old pride begins to show again, his insolent, overbearing smile to return, and Esther, watching him, knows that either she or Haman must fall this day.

Ahasuerus is in a satisfied mood. Never has he sat at a better ordered feast; never has a woman appeared so gracious and lovely in his eyes as Esther, the fair young queen, and he thinks:—

"Today she is to tell me what it is she desires so greatly. Richer and more costly jewels? A greater number of slaves? Fresh palaces, new gardens, stately cities? Nothing in all my wide empire could be too precious a gift to bestow upon Esther, my queen."

And he turns to her, and says:—

"What is thy petition, queen Esther? and it shall be granted thee: and what is thy request? and it shall be performed, even to the half of the kingdom" (Esther 7. 2).

The hour has come. Esther must speak now, or her people must perish.

A solemn light is in her eyes, a passion of prayer in her heart, as she rises to her feet, for the lives of all God's chosen race, scattered throughout the Persian empire, hang upon her next words.

Esther is in favour with the king. He would not allow her to be murdered; and Mordecai's life, too, would be safe at her request, but this will not content her; she will drive all such selfish thoughts far from her mind, she will make herself one with her people, and stand or fall with them.

And the queen throws herself at the king's feet, and with eyes full of tears, and a voice of agonized entreaty, she cries out:—

"If I have found favour in thy sight, O king, and if it please the king, let my life be given me at my petition, and my people at my request" (Esther 7. 3).

Her life? The *queen's* life? The king starts violently on his golden throne—Haman starts violently in his silver seat. The queen's people? Who are they? What is this that is coming upon him?

"For we are sold, I and my people," she sobs, her voice thrilling with grief, the large crystal drops falling fast down her white cheeks, *"to be destroyed, to be slain, and to perish."*

As one overwhelmed with astonishment Ahasuerus gazes on Esther's clasped hands, and pleading face. *She*—his beautiful, beloved queen, asking for her life, and the lives of her people? Who in all the broad earth would dare to threaten the life of his queen?

"But if we had been sold for bondmen and bondwomen, I had held my tongue, although the enemy could not countervail the king's damage," she cries.

Slavery, bonds, she would have submitted to without a murmur—she, the queen? She is asking only for the right to breathe, only for life—life!

But the king cries out in sudden, fierce anger:—

"Who is he, and where is he, that durst presume in his heart to do so?"

Better for a man to have never been born than to fall into a tyrant's hands when wrath like this is flashing from his eyes, when tones of such ungoverned fury are echoing in his voice!

—   —   —

There is a moment's dreadful silence, as Esther rises to her feet. One frail woman, she stands alone between the Jewish people and their doom.

But the light of a high and noble courage glitters in her eyes as she stands there; her tears cease to flow; she looks every inch a queen.

She has made no accusation against Haman as yet; she has said no word behind his back; she has uttered no artful whisper; she has taken no mean advantage. No, she has kept silence; and now at last, when she is forced to speak, she does so, in all honesty and straightforward dealing, before his face.

"The adversary and enemy is this wicked Haman," she says, in low, intense tones, and stretches out her hand towards him.

Haman cowers before that pointing finger as though it were an arrow aimed at his heart, and the faintness of mortal terror falls upon him.

But Ahasuerus' face is aflame on the instant, and the fury of his rage almost chokes him. He cannot speak, he cannot breathe for passion; he must have air—air!

He rises hastily from his throne of gold, his white and purple robes sweeping round him, and passes through the curtained door of the "house of the women" into the green cool of the garden-grove beyond. •

Half-dazed, the wretched Haman sees him go, and a faint hope revives in his heart. The king has pronounced no judgment upon him: there is yet time to plead for his life.

The queen! Yes, she is merciful; she has not asked for his punishment; she does not wish for revenge—Oh, if she would speak for him to the king!

He drags himself to his feet, *"and stands up to make request for his life to Esther the queen; for he saw that there was evil determined against him by the king."*

But ere Esther can speak, and just as Haman's limbs, half-paralysed with terror, fail beneath him, and he falls, almost fainting, at her feet, the king returns, and his anger thunders forth.

Then do the waiting chamberlains draw a covering over Haman's face, for they see that he is already condemned.

Amongst many of the ancient nations, it was the custom to cover a man's face when he was condemned to death, as a sign that he was no longer worthy to look upon the light.

Many slaves stand in the hall. Many who have fawned on Haman, flattered him, grovelled at his feet as though he was more than man. Amongst the crowd of chamberlains and servants is there not one to pity him, not one to sorrow for his disgrace, his deep distress?

No, not one. Stay, Harbonah, the king's chamberlain, is about to speak;—Harbonah, one of the seven chamberlains whom Ahasuerus sent to summon Queen Vashti to his

• The plan of "Shushan the palace," given on page 47 shows this door to the garden quite clearly.

presence, in the days when Esther lived, a humble maid, in the house of Mordecai.

Harbonah knows all the ways of the court. He is a trusted servant, and understands the king's temper well. With a sidelong glance out of his narrow eyes at Haman's cowering figure, he says softly:—

"Behold also, the gallows fifty cubits high, which Haman had made for Mordecai, who had spoken good for the king, standeth in the house of Haman."

The king's eyes flash with cruel joy; the cunning suggestion just suits his humour, as Harbonah guessed it would. Haman erected a stake on which to hang one of the Royal Benefactors?—he shall perish by his own work!

Then cries the king:—

"Hang him thereon!"

Then is the king's signet—the sign of his power taken from Haman, and he is led away to die. Led back to the court of his own fine house, where he has lorded it so long; where he has boasted so often of his glory and riches; where he has planned and carried through so many cruel deeds.

The dreadful stake stands ready, the executioners are there; the fate that he designed for Mordecai has fallen on himself. In that thought lies the bitterest sting of all. This is the end of his boundless ambition, his pride, his cruelty!

He casts one wild look round him. Of all the hundreds of faces gathered to look upon his shame and agony not one is softened with a pitying glance; no tears are shed, no mourning made for him.

Notwithstanding his mighty opportunity, Haman has done no useful work; no man or woman in all the world has cause to bless his name. He lived but for himself, and he goes, unregretted, to his shameful grave. "His mischief has returned upon his own head." "He made a pit, and digged it and is fallen into the ditch which he made" (Psalm 7. 15).

In the day of his greatest power, in the very hour of his triumph and splendour, God's hand touched him, and he became as a handful of dust blown away by the wind.

Until Haman is dead no one dares to approach the king. The eyes of Ahasuerus are opened at last, and he is well-nigh mad with anger to think how Haman has played upon him, used him to obtain his own wicked ends. How weak he has been to believe all Haman's flattering speeches, how foolish to be guided by the advice of a heartless, self-seeking man!

While Haman yet lives he feels an intolerable sense of disgrace. At last word is brought that the "Jews' enemy" is dead. Henceforth that is the name by which Haman will be remembered. *"Then was the king's wrath pacified"* (Esther 7. 10).

His good humour returns; he begins to think of Esther, his beloved queen. Haman has caused her much grief and anxiety; he would comfort her with some splendid gift.

Many times has Ahasuerus offered Esther rich gifts—*even to the half of his kingdom;* but she has taken nothing for herself, and he thinks:—

"Haman was for ever gathering riches; gold and slaves, and costly garments. Esther the queen asks for none of these things: it is fair and just that Haman's house and all his great possessions should be given into her hands." [*]

With modest grace, and grateful thanks, Esther receives the king's splendid gift. Well pleased, Ahasuerus speaks of Mordecai, the Royal Benefactor, whom Haman wished to kill. What shall be done for him?

Then, in her sweet, low tones, Esther tells who Mordecai is, and all he has been to her. How he had taken her into his house, an orphan maid, and loved and cared for her as his own daughter.

Ahasuerus does nothing by halves; his passionate nature flies quickly from one extreme to another. In a fury of wrath but a few hours ago, he is now in the kindest and most generous of tempers.

"Mordecai, my sweet queen's cousin? Mordecai the faithful watcher who saved my life; Mordecai, who resisted the pride of that wicked —Go! my chamberlains, bring Mordecai the Jew

[*] On the death of a condemned man in Persia all his property returned to the king.

hither to me, that I may fittingly reward him."

From his humble seat at the king's gate Mordecai is brought into the gorgeous hall where Ahasuerus sits on his golden throne. The king looks keenly at him. What a contrast to Haman! How brave and steady his voice; how calm and wise his face and expression.

"This is a man I can trust! This is a man who will help me to rule my empire wisely and well!" thinks Ahasuerus, and he takes the signet, the sign of his authority, torn a few hours since from the wretched Haman, and puts it into Mordecai's hands. *

While Haman possessed the king's seal he had almost all the king's power; now Mordecai, the patient, faithful Jew, who has endured so bravely, who trusted in the God of his fathers, and resisted the wicked Haman even to death, stands next to Ahasuerus, the ruler of the greatest empire in the world.

Then comes Queen Esther also, her beautiful eyes shining with love and gratitude. The king has given her Haman's house; she may not give away the king's gift; but she can use it as she pleases. Mordecai is to be chief officer of State in Haman's place, and Esther has determined that he shall have Haman's house also.

"When I was a poor friendless girl he took me into his house and comforted me," she thinks—"now it is my turn"; and so she gives him a palace to live in, keeping back nothing of all Haman's riches for herself.

But in a little while all Esther's and Mordecai's joy and thankfulness are again turned to mourning and cruel anxiety. They had thought the battle won; their nation saved. They find, to their grief and horror, that the people are in as great danger as ever.

Alas! the evil done by a wicked man does not end with his life.

Now, indeed, the case seems hopeless; for the laws of Persia make mercy impossible. Mordecai, all anxiety to get the cruel order against the Jews recalled, is met with the stern words,

* Persian kings did not *sign* State documents, they *sealed* them. Thousands of ancient signets have been found in the ruins of great cities of old times.

"That which has once been decreed in the king's name must stand for ever."

All his new power is of no avail! Wise, devoted though he is, Mordecai can do nothing.

"The king is as a god," say the Persians; "the gods cannot change, nor their decrees be swept away; neither can the king's. The decree was written in the king's name, and it must stand."

Then does a passion of grief and despair seize on Esther's heart that all care for her own life, all remembrance of her dignity, is swept away. *She* is safe in the king's love, Mordecai in the king's friendship, but this knowledge brings to her no comfort.

Against all the customs of the court she hurries to the king— she quite forgets now the risk she is running. She *fell down at his feet, and besought him with tears to put away the mischief of Haman the Agagite, and his device that he had devised against the Jews"* (Esther 8. 3).

She thinks only of her people, sold to slaughter. She is their voice. She is speaking for those who cannot speak for themselves. She is pleading for those who stand on the verge of destruction.

The king holds his golden sceptre towards her, and she rises and stands before him, wringing her hands in extremest sorrow.

"If it please the king, and if I have found favour in his sight, and the thing seem right before the king, and I be pleasing in his eyes"—how hard she pleads—how thrilling her voice—how deep the entreaty in her great, dark eyes!—*"let it be written to reverse the letters devised by Haman."*

Wise Esther! She is trying to make the king see that this wicked decree was *Haman's* act, not his— *"which HE wrote to destroy the Jews which are in all the king's provinces. For how can I endure to see the evil that shall come unto my people? or how can I endure to see the destruction of my kindred?"*

Alas! alas! have all her prayers, struggles, tears, fastings, been in vain? Sobs choke her voice; she can say no more.

11

THE SECOND DECREE

Ahasuerus is deeply touched and stirred by his beloved queen's agonised pleading, the bitter tears; but in his heart he thinks, "What can I do that I have not already done?"

He looks long at Esther's drooping figure, trembling with sobs; he glances at the pale, troubled face of Mordecai. How can he help them? How save their people, whilst the decree sent forth in his name remains against them?

Of course that decree must stand. He is the "great king, the king of the lands where many languages are spoken";* far better that a whole nation should perish than that one word of his should be changed or altered.

But as he ponders over the difficulty the thought comes into his mind, "Mordecai is wise and faithful, perhaps *he* can find a way to help his people—I care not at all what that way is, so that it does not lower my name, or authority, nor the awe and worship in which the nation hold me."

And he says:—

"Behold, I have given Esther the house of Haman, and him they have hanged upon the gallows, because he laid his hand upon the Jews" (Esther 8. 7).

"Haman wrote in my name to destroy the Jews, now I give you leave to save them if you can. *Write ye also for the Jews, as it liketh you, in the king's name, and seal it with the king's ring: for the writing which is written in the king's name and sealed with the king's ring, may no man reverse.*"

---

* These words have been found carved on one of his palaces.

There is no help for it, then. Mordecai has no choice; the decree of death must stand. All he can do is to give his people the right to defend themselves when their enemies come to slay them.

So terrible is the power of Ahasuerus, so completely are the lives of his subjects in his hands, that without this direct leave from the king they would have been expected to allow themselves, their wives and little ones, to be murdered without resistance.

Again the king's scribes are sent for. It is the month of Sivan, that is, May, the beautiful month of flowers; but there is little thought of flowers in Shushan the palace this three-and-twentieth day, for the scribes must work as they have seldom worked before.

Not only are copies of the new decree to be sent *"to the lieutenants, and the deputies and rulers of the provinces which are from India unto Ethiopia,"* each copy written *"unto every people after their language,"* but this time copies are to be put into the hands of the Jews in all the provinces; that they may know what to do, and be ready against the coming of that dreadful day in Adar, the "dark month," when all those who hate them shall come upon them to spoil and slay.

Power to defend themselves; that is all! Leave *"to gather themselves together, and stand for their life."*

True, it is added to the decree, according to the Persian custom of these days, that the Jews may *"take the spoil of them for a prey,"* that is, take the clothes and ornaments of the slain; but, as we shall see, the Jews have no mind to spoil their enemies, no thought of gain mingles with their prayers. The right to live! This is all Esther has pleaded for, all that Mordecai is striving to secure.

How sad that Mordecai should be forced to send out such a decree as this; how terrible that a great king would rather plunge his people into civil war than be ready to own he had made a mistake!

And Mordecai writes *"in the King Ahasuerus' name, and*

sealed it with the king's ring, and sent letters by posts on horseback" (Esther 8. 10).

This account agrees exactly with the description of the Persian posts found in Herodotus. He explains that Ahasuerus—or "Xerxes," as the Greeks call him—was in the habit of sending important news by horse-posts. "Nothing mortal travels so fast as the Persian messenger-posts," he remarks. "The first rider delivers his dispatches to the second, stationed a day's journey up the road; the second to the third, and so on along the whole line." We read, too, in the old histories, that the king had a special breed of horses, "bred of the stud" for the "posts," while Persian riders were famous throughout the world.

Away, away they flew, down all the high roads of Persia; over plain and mountain, by night and by day. Hasten—hasten! Faster and faster yet! Press on, stay not for burning sun, or blinding rain—on, on, by command of the king!

Thus is the news of the king's new decree *"published unto all people that the Jews should be ready."*

Grief and deep despair are in the cities which lie ahead of the messengers, but hope and thankful hearts in those they have left behind!

"Oh, wonderful, this is the Lord's doing! He has not forsaken His people. Haman had thought to destroy us, but God has overruled his evil purpose. Oh, give thanks unto the Lord, the Holy One of Israel!"

And all the best and most enlightened people of Persia rejoice with their Jewish neighbours; for there are many who, though they do not know God by His true name, believe in One Creator, and respect the Jew's religion.

Truly grieved were these good citizens at Haman's cruel order; and now, that the second decree is published, they side openly with the Jews, and against their heathen fellow-subjects—the men and women who worship idols, who sacrifice to devils, who are looking forward with savage joy to the day when they may shed the Jew's blood like water, and fill the streets of their towns with the bodies of the slain.

"And in every province, and in every city, whithersoever the king's commandment and his decree came, the Jews had joy and gladness, a feast and a good day. And many of the people of the land became Jews."

And Mordecai, whose features have been so often bathed in sorrow; whose head has been sprinkled with ashes, and his limbs clad in sackcloth; whose heart so lately seemed ready to break beneath its load of grief—Mordecai goes *"out from the presence of the king in royal apparel of blue and white, and with a great crown of gold, and with a garment of fine linen and purple"* (Esther 8. 15).

Blue, purple, white—the royal colours of Persia. Great nobles and faithful officers are allowed to adorn their heads with a crown. Crowns are a sign of the king's favour and confidence; that is all. *

Hark! What is that?

The sun is setting over Shushan the palace; but the still evening air is filled with the murmur of many voices rising loud from "Shushan the city."

The new decree has just been published. Haman's dread order of death was received in saddened silence by the most enlightened citizens, in perplexity by all.

Mordecai listens intently.

"Oh, thanks be to God, we have many friends, the people of Shushan are shouting for joy!"

—   —   —

As the "dark" month draws nearer and nearer, as the day of death approaches, the people throughout the whole empire become gradually divided into two camps—those who mean to attack, who are eager to shed blood, who long to break into houses, to kill, and destroy, to carry off all the goods they can lay their hands on; and those who think only of defending their dear ones, who hope for no gain, who think neither of silver

---

* On a wall of the British Museum, just behind the great human headed winged lions from Assyria, are some fragments of carvings from one of Ahasuerus' palaces. Quite a number of the figures are wearing crowns.

nor gold, cattle nor goods, who ask only that their wives, their little children, may be allowed to live.

But will the Jews' enemies attack now? Is it not known throughout all the land that the king does not wish the Jews to suffer—that the good and beautiful young queen is herself a Jewess?

The Jews will not attack; this second decree is quite unlike the first. It gives the Jews no power but the right of defence.

Surely the heathen people will hesitate, will draw back?

Ah, no, no! The worshippers of false gods learn to love slaughter; they are greedy after spoil. Haman's wicked decree has given them just the opportunity they longed for. They will make full and fearful use of it. Massacres have no terror for the subjects of King Ahasuerus. Indeed, this will not be the first time they have been engaged in one.

We have already heard, in an earlier chapter, of one terrible massacre in Persia. It occurred in the reign of Darius, the father of Ahasuerus. On a set day, all the Magians who could be found were killed, the day being kept for many years afterwards as a national holiday.

Herodotus, the Greek historian, tells us that on another occasion the Persian monarch, having had trouble with a wild tribe of people, called them together and invited the greater part to a festival. He waited until they were helpless with wine, and then ordered his servants to massacre them all.

So *"the Jews gather themselves together in their cities, throughout all the provinces of the King Ahasuerus."*

"Shoulder to shoulder, fellow-countrymen! For our homes, for the lives of our children! Oh, brothers, fathers, sons, the time draws very near."

So cry the young men, but the old men make answer:—

"Take comfort, people of Israel, Mordecai the Jew is very great. Haman was despised and hated even in the day of his glory, but throughout the whole land men are speaking of Mordecai's wisdom and power; for his sake, throughout the whole land, the king's officers are our friends, and will send no soldiers against us. Ah, is not this a sure sign that the Lord is with His people still?"

So in Shushan, in Babylon the old, in Ectabana the beautiful, and in many a city more, the Jews are banded together.

It is the time of dawn—a cold and cheerless dawn in the "dark" month, in the winter of the year.

Sadly the wan light breaks over the plains of Shushan, over the brown roofs of the city, the tiled halls and marble pillars of the palace on the hill.

Ah, the people are early astir. See, already the streets are full of hurrying figures, are echoing with the hoarse murmur of angry voices; yes, and the ring of armour, and the sharp clashing of swords and spears!

Only in the Jews' quarter all is silent. The house doors and window-shutters fast closed, the outer courts deserted. But behind those barred gates what anxious hearts are beating, what eager ears are strained to catch every sound, what passionate prayers are poured out from lips white as death!

"The twelfth month, the thirteenth day of the month. Oh, mothers, clasp your children close! Oh, children, to your knees, and entreat the Lord to save your lives this day! Hark! hark! my brothers, do they come?"

They come! Fierce cries, the tramp of myriad feet, the crash of doors furiously beaten in, the flash of lifted sword, and ready spear. Ah, what a hell upon earth has King Ahasuerus made of Shushan the city and Shushan the palace this day!

But *"the Jews smite all their enemies with the stroke of the sword."*

Those who are hungry to shed the innocent blood fall victims to their own fury. These ten sons of Haman, who rage up and down the streets, urging their followers on to deeds of desperate cruelty, crying to them to slay all—all—men, women, and little children—they are themselves slain at last; and the night falls and the dreadful day is over.

"And in Shushan the palace"—that is, on the great mound, where numbers of buildings besides the palace are clustered together—*"the Jews slay and destroy five hundred men."*

The king's decree included women and children, but the men of Israel have no warfare with women and babes—it is the *men* only who can slay their dear ones.

Rich jewels, gold, fine clothes—what are these to them? They are not fighting for gain—let the women whose husbands they have been compelled to slay, let the children, whose fathers have fallen into the pit they digged for others, take the spoil. "As for us, we will have none of it."

So unusual was this generous conduct in those days that the historian evidently thought it a most wonderful sign of the purity of the Jews' intentions, and, therefore, repeats it three times *(see verses 10, 15, 16),* that there may be no mistake.

Then do the king's scribes go through all the streets, making out lists of the slain; this they must always do after battle or massacre; and the lists are brought to the king.

"And the king says unto Esther the queen, The Jews have slain and destroyed five hundred men in Shushan the palace, and the ten sons of Haman; what have they done in the rest of the king's provinces?"

Yet, alas! all is not over. So furious are the Jews' enemies, that there is but too much reason to fear they will overstep the bounds of the first decree, defy the king, and attack the Jews again directly morning breaks.

Something must be done, and that quickly; therefore the king says:—

"Now, what is thy petition? and it shall be granted thee, or what is thy request further? and it shall be done."

Very pale is Esther the queen as she makes answer. The Jews in the provinces are safe. But in Shushan are many of Haman's friends as wicked as he was himself; in Shushan Haman's sons have stirred the evil passions of the heathen people into madness. Too well she sees that, unless her countrymen have leave to defend their homes this second day also, all will have been in vain.

"If it please the king, let it be granted to the Jews which are in Shushan, to do to-morrow also according unto this day's decree."

Then a wise thought comes to her; whether prompted by Mordecai, the wise ruler, or not, we are not told.

Eastern people have no heart to fight after the death of their leaders. Haman's sons, to whom the Jews' enemies look naturally, are slain. What better way of cooling the furious rage of the heathen, and thus save further slaughter, than by showing them at a glance that their leaders are dead?

"And let Haman's ten sons be hanged upon the gallows." •

Wise, merciful Esther! The maddened people must believe their own eyes. No way so sure as this for bringing peace to the troubled land!

• Herodotus tells us that Ahasuerus was in the habit of hanging up the bodies of conquered generals, as a sign that the war was ended.

12

ESTHER'S DECREE

It is over. The hoarse shouts of the attackers, the groans of the wounded have died away into silence.

A second day of horror has passed over Shushan. The Jews' enemies, frantic with baffled spite, again break in upon the watchful Jews, sword in hand, crying out that they would kill and destroy every man, woman, and child among them.

It has been just as Esther and Mordecai feared; but the riot had ceased at last. Dismay has fallen on the Jews' enemies; the idol-worshippers have gone down before the people who trust in the God of Israel.

But this fourteenth day of Adar, so terrible in Shushan, has been bright with joy and thanksgiving throughout all the other cities and villages of Persia. Shushan has been the one dark spot in a world of sunshine.

Weary, dispirited, last night found the heathen in the king's provinces everywhere too disheartened to break the king's edict, and continue the struggle.

Besides, the Jews had taken nothing from them—not one piece of money, nor a single jewel. "Best leave things as they are, lest worse befall us," thought the heathen.

So, whilst yet the black storm of strife was hanging over Shushan, whilst its walls yet rang to the direful sounds of the deadly struggle raging within, the walls and towers of distant towns were echoing back the glad music of psalms of thanksgiving.

What shouts of joy went up! The streets were filled with happy crowds—the Jews and the Jews' friends rejoicing together. But the Jews' enemies kept quietly within their houses.

"Ah, what a glorious victory the Lord has given His people! Yesterday, we stood for our lives and the lives of our little ones; in doubt we stood—in deep anguish; but the Lord was with us, and He has turned our mourning into joy!"

"But the Jews that were in Shushan assembled together on the thirteenth day thereof, and on the fourteenth day thereof; and on the fifteenth day of the same they rested, and made it a day of feasting and gladness" (Esther 9. 18).

So, though all the Jews have escaped the same terrible destruction, though all have stood together like brothers in that awful struggle for the very existence of their nation, they are now divided in their thanksgiving to God!

"The Jews of the villages that dwell in the unwalled towns" must keep the fourteenth day of the month as a day of thankfulness to the Lord, and of charity and love to one another.

Oh, how can they ever forget that on this day the cruel anxiety, the sickening fear, was lifted from their hearts? From the grey-haired elders, down to the toddling infants, this fourteenth day of Adar must be sacred for evermore!

Yet how can the Jews of Shushan make that second black day of slaughter *their* day of thanksgiving and gladness?

Those fearful hours of struggle are full of bitter memories—a day of fasting, of wailing, of death at their very doors.

"But that day in which the terror and the shame were taken from us, when our soul rejoiced in the Lord, and our hearts were filled with His praise—the fifteenth day, the day of rest—Ah, that we must remember, and our children after us, as long as our nation shall endure!"

Here, indeed, is a difficult question for Mordecai to settle! The queen and himself feel most strongly that a special time of thanksgiving should be set apart, to be observed year by year, as a perpetual memorial of God's great mercy to their nation.

"A national rejoicing should be kept by all sections of the

nation together," he says. And it shall be so kept!

"Rejoice, my people—pour out your hearts in thanksgivings on both days! Are not we all brothers? Hundreds of miles may divide us, but we are all one people; we have all passed through the same danger. God has given to us all the same glorious triumph. Let those of us who dwell in Shushan rejoice on the fourteenth day, remembering that at this time their brethren in the cities and villages of many lands, far away across the plains of Shushan, and beyond the rugged mountains, had rest from their enemies; and let those in all the provinces be glad on the morrow—thanksgiving day of their brethren of Shushan."

"And Mordecai wrote these things, and sent letters unto all the Jews that were in all the provinces of the king Ahasuerus, both nigh and far, to stablish this among them, that they should keep the fourteenth day of the month Adar, and the fifteenth day of the same, yearly" (Esther 9. 20, 21).

"Fellow-countrymen, on these days let us be brothers indeed. Let us share our goods with those who are in need, let us remember the widow and the fatherless, for in these days we had rest from our enemies, our mourning was turned to good, and our sorrow to joy, therefore let them be *days of feasting and joy, and of sending portions one to another, and gifts to the poor."*

A noble way this, indeed, of celebrating a great victory!

A national thanksgiving. A time of rejoicing for evermore. The whole nation welcomes it gladly.

But a great festival like this must have a name. What shall these days be called?

Then do the Jews think over the long series of events that have led to their deliverance. This special time of year had been set apart for their destruction because Haman had *"cast Pur, that is, the lot,"* until the twelfth month had appeared.

How wonderfully God had brought it about, that the very day fixed for their massacre should be the time of their most splendid triumph! They must never forget how God overruled the day of Pur—the lot.

"Wherefore they call these days Purim, after the name of Pur."

"Never shall they be forgotten! Never will we allow the remembrance of God's mercy to fade from our minds! Never will we fail to raise our voices in prayer and praise in the days of Purim *throughout every generation, every family, every province, every city; these days of Purim shall not fail from among the Jews, nor the memorial of them perish from their seed."*

Esther the queen is a strong power in the State now. Ahasuerus at last understands something of her wisdom and goodness, and she moves throughout Shushan the palace a queen in power and authority, as well as in name.

Many decrees have been sent in the king's name from Shushan; now one goes forth in the name of Esther the queen.

"Esther the queen, the daughter of Abihail"—so she writes to her people—"Your queen and your countrywoman," *"and Mordecai the Jew, write with all authority to confirm the second letter of Purim."*

Yes, and to do more than that: to bid them remember *'the matters of the fastings and their cry."*

"Forget not, Oh, my people, in your rejoicings, the fastings and cryings; forget not the greatness of your deliverance; keep the remembrance of God's mercy continually before you!"

Four great decrees have we seen sent out. The decree of Ahasuerus, sending Vashti into banishment and disgrace. Haman's decree of slaughter. The decree that followed, allowing civil war.

The fourth decree, *"the decree of Esther,"* is indeed different from all the others.

"Remember your deliverance; rejoice; send food to the hungry; give gifts to the poor."

This is a decree of thanksgiving, charity, peace, and love. The decree of a true woman, a great leader, a noble queen.

So the decree of Esther stands to this day. The Jews are saved, the struggle over, the victory sure.

So much we know of Esther, and the work God gave her to

do; but what befell her next, and how she died at last we know not at all.

"And the King Ahasuerus laid a tribute upon the land, and upon the isles of the sea" (Esther 10. 1).

Ahasuerus was king of a very great country, but he was not a great king. He could tax whom he pleased, but he could not rule himself. Terrible as was his name in his own days, it is despised now; and though his subjects treated him as more than man, we know that he was a vain and cruel tyrant.

It was his father Darius who first taxed the "isles of the sea." In Herodotus there is a long account of the different sums of money each nation is to pay. Afterwards, this arrangement had to be altered. Ahasuerus lost a number of the "isles of the sea" (islands in the Mediterranean Sea) through his own pride and wilfulness.

Afterwards, he built many great palaces— *"acts of power and might"*—but now they are dust and heaps of broken stones. He founded great cities, of which nothing remains but the names. The gardens he planted are deserts. His broad fields, once rich with corn and fruit, are sandy wastes.

In his day his power and might were greater than those of any earthly king, but his glory has long since passed away, and been forgotten.

Haman, the "wicked Haman," is not forgotten. Still is he known as the "Jews' enemy." Still, whenever a Jew, who is true to his nation, hears Haman's name spoken, he cries, "May his name be blotted out!" Haman's cruelty and vain-glory, and his fearful fall will never be forgotten.

The tyrant is despised; Haman detested; but among the children of his people, Mordecai is more loved and honoured than ever; more than he was in those far away days, when *'the declaration of the greatness of Mordecai, whereunto the king advanced him, are they not written in the book of the chronicles of the kings of Media and Persia?"* (Esther 10.2).

He has always been so honoured. His name has been a household word to the Jews for generations. From time to time in ancient histories, we find mention of his name; and the great feast of Purim, which is sometimes called "Mordecai's Day."

These words occur in the history of Josephus, written eighteen hundred years ago:—

"The Jews still keep the days of Purim. Mordecai became a great and illustrious person with the king, and assisted him in the government of the people. He also abode with the queen, so the affairs of the Jews were better than they could have hoped for."

How wonderfully God brought this about! A humble watchman, condemned to a disgraceful death, becomes the most powerful ruler in a mighty kingdom, and so earns the gratitude of his people that his name is remembered and honoured to this day!

*"Mordecai the Jew was next unto King Ahasuerus, and great among the Jews, and accepted of the multitude of his brethren, seeking the wealth * of his people, and speaking peace to all his seed"* (Esther 10. 3).

"Words of peace and truth" spoken to them (Esther 9. 30). Their peace and prosperity his constant care. No wonder the name of Mordecai is blessed among his people still!

But the name of Esther is given to one of the books of the Bible, as you all know. While this world lasts shall her name be remembered.

Yet, when first she was taken to the king's palace she was but a simple young girl. She did not wish to go. One old tradition says she cried bitterly at the thought of leaving home.

But see what a position she took up at once! Sparkling jewels, richly embroidered dresses, were offered to her. She explained that she had no need of such things.

The palace of a Persian king was a perfect hotbed of quarrelling and jealousy. Yet so gentle, so unselfish and true was Esther that even these selfish, worldly people all learnt to love her before her year of waiting was out.

The king chose her for his queen, but splendour in which she was obliged to live did not make her forget her foster-father,

Wealth—*good*—r.v.

nor the duty she owed him. She took care to be informed of all that happened to him.

Had Esther neglected Mordecai, the chamberlain would never have thought to tell her of the grief of a humble watchman; and she, perhaps, had not known, until too late, the awful doom that was coming on her people.

Then came the great moment of her life. The gentle girl must make a bold stand; must dare death itself in pleading the cause of her people.

"Death! Ah, death is better than to keep silence when my people are on the eve of destruction: *so will I go in unto the king, which is not according to the law; and if I perish, I perish.*"

Think of Esther's words, all you who are hesitating about doing what your conscience tells you is right.

What is the very worst that can happen, after all, if you do your duty? Face it out. Count the cost, as Esther did, and be ready as she was to pay the price!

More than two thousand years have rolled away since Esther lived. Generations on generations have been born and died; the splendid palace in which she dwelt has crumbled into a heap of dust. Shushan the city has vanished; the river that wound about its walls in Esther's days is choked with reeds and rubbish; the beautiful groves and gardens of Shushan are no more. Only the wide plains, and the distant mountains, towards which Esther must have looked so often—sometimes in grief and perplexity, sometimes in joy—remain of the same shapes and colours as in the days of old, when Shushan the palace was the most beautiful building in the whole world.

Deep in the earth they found, not long ago, a tomb in Shushan. Golden bracelets and clasps, such as queens wore in Esther's days, lay within it, and besides them a few handfuls of dust, and the bones of a woman.

We know not the name of this woman; but just so would Esther have been laid to rest, just so would her tomb appear today.

So long ago she lived, so long ago she died. Yet the memory of what she did, her courage, her self-sacrifice, her wisdom, and her love, will live for ever.

Never has her decree been broken, nor her words forgotten. Still on every return of Adar, the "dark" month, is the feast of Purim kept by the people of her nation. Still do the scattered families of the Jews—once God's chosen people—meet each succeeding year in their synagogues on the two days appointed by Esther and Mordecai.

Then is the Megillah—that is 'roll'—of Esther taken reverently from its resting-place, and solemnly read aloud; the people following the beautiful history with closest attention.

"The Lord is on my side; I will not fear: what can man do unto me?"

That was Esther's trust. Let it be ours. Strong in faith and purity, let us go forward with confidence. Oh, for men and women today who are ready to trust their God and act upon their convictions like Esther the queen!